The Making of
Dr. C.
A Memoir
Dr. Cassundra White-Elliott

This is a work of non-fiction, written from the author's memory. Some details may not align with other persons' memory of shared events, but the author shares the events from her memory and/or the memory of others who shared specific details with her in times past. Most names have been omitted, while other names have been changed, to protect identities.

Included scripture are from various versions of the Holy Bible, primarily King James version, except where noted.

CLF Publishing, LLC.
www.clfpublishing.org

Cover design by Senir Design. Contact information: info@senirdesign.com.

ISBN # 978-1-945102-32-5

Printed in the United States of America.

Acknowledgements

I acknowledge everyone who helped me celebrate this year of jubilee and all God's blessings!

Dedication

To my granddaughter, my mini-me,

Kimara Tsehai Faith White

Always remember who you are!

You can do all things through Christ Jesus!

Never stop believing in yourself!

Dr. C. White-Elliott

Dr. C. White-Elliott

Table of Contents

Introduction

A baby girl is born through the natural process of being delivered from her mother's womb, either vaginally or by Cesarean. After she has breathed in the very elixir of life and air has filled her lungs, from that moment forward, every experience, thought, and deed begins to shape the woman she will eventually become, thus demonstrating the sum total of her experiences combined with the spiritual, emotional, and intellectual awakening.

As she walks onto the stage called "Life," she begins to perform as she is nurtured, coached, prodded, twisted, and turned. Every act of love and kindness she experiences, as well as every instance of abuse she may suffer, will shape her psyche and dictate the actions she will eventually execute and the words she will utter. And no ever one knows what lies behind her pretty face. One moment she may present a gentle smile, and in a split second, a wicked laugh can escape through those same lips.

The Making of Dr. C. is an unveiling of the inner workings of God's chosen vessel: Dr. Cassundra Lynett (Flemister) White-Elliott. The pages of this memoir will reveal the process she had to undergo to evolve into the woman she is today. It is a demonstration of God's power and a celebration of 50 years in the making.

Now, she anxiously anticipates what God has yet in store for her and what He is going to do next!

"All The World's A Stage"

By William Shakespeare

(from As You Like It*, spoken by Jaques)*

All the world's a stage,
And all the men and women merely players;
They have their exits and their entrances;
And one man in his time plays many parts,
His acts being seven ages. At first the infant,
Mewling and puking in the nurse's arms;
And then the whining school-boy, with his satchel
And shining morning face, creeping like snail
Unwillingly to school. And then the lover,
Sighing like furnace, with a woeful ballad
Made to his mistress' eyebrow. Then a soldier,
Full of strange oaths, and bearded like the pard,
Jealous in honour, sudden and quick in quarrel,
Seeking the bubble reputation
Even in the cannon's mouth. And then the justice,
In fair round belly with good capon lin'd,
With eyes severe and beard of formal cut,
Full of wise saws and modern instances;
And so he plays his part. The sixth age shifts
Into the lean and slipper'd pantaloon,
With spectacles on nose and pouch on side;
His youthful hose, well sav'd, a world too wide
For his shrunk shank; and his big manly voice,
Turning again toward childish treble, pipes
And whistles in his sound. Last scene of all,
That ends this strange eventful history,
Is second childishness and mere oblivion;
Sans teeth, sans eyes, sans taste, sans everything.

Dr. C.

My Grand Entrance

ACT I

After Sunday, June 30, 1968, the world would forever be changed because I had officially made my footprint that would mark out time for a predestined number of years that only God Almighty is privy. Job 14:1 says, *"Man that is born of a woman is of few days and full of trouble,"* and Job 14:5 says, *"Seeing his days are determined, the number of his months are with thee, thou hast appointed his bounds that he cannot pass."*

Prior to my birth, I was destined to take the world by force and deposit into it love, laughter, compassion, understanding, knowledge, and wisdom. Jeremiah 1:5 says, *"Before I formed thee in the belly I knew thee; and before thou camest forth out of the womb I sanctified thee, and I ordained thee a prophet unto the nations."* So, the Lord knew me before He drew me from my mother's womb, and He had a specific plan for my life.

However, unbeknownst to me, in the midst of God's plan, fear, anger, bewilderment, disappointment, and grief were added to the equation. The way my life would unfold would not only surprise those closest to me, but the surprises (both welcome and unwelcome) would shake me to my very core, causing not only a rude awakening surrounded by regret, but also moments of pleasure, happiness, joy, fulfillment, and wonder were deposited as well.

From my description, you can probably imagine my life being similar to a dangerous, yet exhilarating roller coaster ride. If you can imagine how it would feel to take such a ride, imagine how the experience was for me to actually live through it. However, the ride would have proven to be smoother if I had been aware to keep in mind the words in Jeremiah 29:11: *"'For I know the plans I have for you,' declares the LORD, 'plans to prosper you and not to harm you, plans to give you hope and a future'"* (NIV).

Unfortunately, I cannot tell the entire existence of all my experiences, but I will give the nuts and bolts.

On Sunday, June 30, 1968, I was born to Noah Alexander Flemister and Gloria Louise Flemister at Fort Bragg Army Base in Fayetteville, North Carolina. A family of three became a family of four. A year and one and a half months prior to my birth, my parents were blessed with a son, who is my darling older brother. We remained stationed at the base for three months. I am not sure where we traveled to afterward, but my parents' permanent residence was in Arkansas, having lived in both Pine Bluff and Little Rock.

However, a season of trouble fell over the family, causing a rift. The family of four split into two parties. One party consisted of one member, and the other party consisted of three. In 1971, the larger party moved to California. However, they were not alone. In 1970, a year, one month, and one day after my birthday, another son had been added. The party of three was then a party of four.

In California, we met up with my maternal grandmother. Eventually, we (the party of four) settled into a two-bedroom apartment. My first memory at three years old is of 1971, the year we moved to California. I have no memory of living anywhere else or of my father, so I can only share what I was told.

I recall having good times with my two brothers at the apartment. On occasion, as nightfall neared, my brothers and I would play in the back of the apartment building, which was actually the parking lot. On one particular evening, I was playing with one of my brother's Tonka trucks. I was on my knees while rolling the truck on the ground.

Suddenly, the truck jerked forward, slipping from my grasp. I tried desperately to hold onto the small vehicle. Before I knew it, my body fell forward, and my face fell to the asphalt pavement, which was very rough. While attempting to keep the truck in my small hand, my face scraped against the asphalt. Needless to say, I scrambled to my feet and immediately went to my mother who was inside the apartment.

Viewing my tear-stained, bruised face, she was not thrilled. Nevertheless, she went right into action while asking what had occurred. She pulled out her medical supplies that all good mothers keep on hand. She commenced to cleaning my face. However, there was no amount of cleaning that could have prevented my eye from turning black as a result of the damaged blood vessels. So, there I was a three-year-old little girl with a black eye.

Unfortunately, that wasn't the only time I would suffer bruising. The Tonka truck incident was innocent. The second incident was due to my mischievousness. When I was approximately ten or eleven years old, my brothers and I were playing and skating at a neighborhood park we frequented on the weekend. While we were there enjoying ourselves, the ice cream truck made its customary visit. After ordering and receiving our treats, I, along with another child, decided to climb onto the rear bumper of the ice cream truck. I had seen that done by several children on other occasions, and despite numerous warnings by the operator of the truck to refrain, I had been experiencing a growing desire to try it.

Ordinarily, I was not an adventurous child. Neither was I a tomboy. But, certain adventures sparked my curiosity. So, on that day, I conjured up my nerve and jumped onto the back of the ice cream truck. After all the young patrons had made their requests and had snacks in hand, the truck began to move slowly down the street towards the next set of customers. Feeling the wind blowing against my ponytails, I was having a blast.

Shortly after though, panic began to set in. The truck drew closer to the end of the block, and that made me nervous. For one, I was not supposed to be on the back of the truck. And two, I was not supposed to leave the park. Therefore, it was time for me to take action. Instead of waiting for the truck to stop, I jumped. The movement of the truck contrasted with my movement in the opposite direction, causing me to fall to the ground. Upon making contact with the ground, my small body began to roll. Can you imagine a small girl falling to the asphalt from a moving vehicle? Although it happened to me, I can barely fathom the thought. And, it gets worse. Falling wasn't the brunt of my catastrophe. I still had to go home and face my mother and explain to her the mischief in which I had involved myself. There was no one to blame but me.

After falling and then collecting myself, I'm not certain if my brothers and I stayed at the park until our appointed departure time or if we left early due to the injury I had sustained. The approximate year was 1979, and cell phones had not yet been invented. Even if they had, I am most certain I would not have had one in my possession. Furthermore, my siblings and I probably had not considered using a payphone to contact our mother. So, I held my arm and cried all the way home. I could have either been crying from the pain or from fear about what my mother would say or both.

Upon my arrival, filled with panic and uncertainty, I searched for my mother. When she saw my bloodied arm, she too panicked and asked a million questions I'm sure. After learning I had essentially done damage to myself, she scolded me for messing myself up just before our trip to my aunt's home in Arkansas. My right arm had made contact with the asphalt, and the skin had been stripped away, down to the white flesh, showing the holes that once held faint, thin hair.

As the days and weeks passed, my arm began to heal as the scab covered the once visible flesh. The process was very painful. And, I remember favoring my arm as an animal would favor and refrain from using a wounded limb. Years later, the scar remains from the "ice cream truck" debacle. And after my incidents with the Tonka truck and the ice cream truck, I decided to keep my adventurous side to activities I deemed safe.

Now, let's go back to the apartment in Los Angeles. A year or two later, I would begin the adventure of a lifetime: I would begin my formative education. From my sketchy recollection of age four and five, I remember being walked to school by an adult. My older brother was always with us. However, neither of us can remember if we started school at the same time, with me going to pre-K and him to kindergarten or me going to kindergarten and him first grade. Unfortunately, both our mother and grandmother are deceased, so we have no one to ask to gain the accurate details.

What I do recall is this- we both attended Ascot Elementary School. And, I was simply tickled to do so. Attending school opened up another world for me and added a dimension to my existence. Many four and five year olds are terrified to leave their parents to venture into the world of the unknown. I, on the other hand, relished the opportunity to explore academia in its fullness. However, I do not recall much about my explorations at Ascot Elementary. I only recall having that brief experience, which lasted only a year or two.

That same year at Christmas time, I recall having one of the most beautiful Christmas trees, and it was complete with presents galore underneath. One of my gifts was an oversize dollhouse with several levels. It was stunning. And, many young girls would have loved to receive it as a gift or just to have the opportunity to play with it. However, at the same Christmas or another event, perhaps my birthday, I received a school house with little people: a teacher and students. Viewing each toy, the school house paled in comparison to the grandiosity of the dollhouse. However, the school house sparked something within me, and for years, it was my favorite toy. I left dolls and doll houses for the other girls. I desired to be the schoolmaster, the one who held all the knowledge and disseminated it to others.

Of course, I love beauty and glamour as do most women. And, I always present myself at 100% – optimal presentation. However, beauty and glamour are exterior accents. Knowledge and the inner workings of one's mind is what will impact other people's lives and open doors for the individual herself. From that moment to this, I have always preferred the strength of the mind over the beauty of the flesh. But, because both play an important role in our society, I strive to keep both stellar.

Eventually, our stay (as a family of four) in Los Angeles came to an end. My mother married her second husband, and he whisked us all away to a new home: a house in Inglewood on Wilton Place. At that time, I was six years old. In the new neighborhood, I could no longer attend my old school. So, in 1974, for first grade, I was enrolled into a new school, one I would attend for only a year.

The only experience I recall at that school was an issue with my name. The teacher asked me to introduce myself, so I told my classmates, "My name is Cassundra." She stated, "That's a long name for a little girl. How about we call you Cass?" At six years old, I was livid. I promptly told her, "No." Then, she inquired about my middle name. When I told her my middle name is Lynett, she wanted to shorten it to Lynn. You wasn't having that either. So, she stuck with Cassundra although I'm sure she pronounced it as Cassandra, instead of with a "u" as in "sun." That was and still is my number one pet peeve. Arhhh! Why the world at large cannot seem to pronounce my name phonetically is a mystery to me. Humph!

In 1975, my family transitioned into a family of six persons (mother, older brother, younger brother, new baby brother, myself, and an unreasonably strict stepfather, who I later experienced firsthand as a pedophile). We moved to a larger house in the city of Carson, onto Denwall Drive. With the move came a new school: Broadacres Elementary School. I attended Broadacres from second grade to six grade. My second grade teacher was Miss Claire. I recall bits and pieces of second grade, but there was nothing I would designate as impactful.

However, third grade with Mrs. Joan Coleman was life changing. First of all, I was enamored by her natural beauty and full head of hair that appeared to be very soft like the clouds. Mrs. Coleman did not possess the figure of a supermodel, but her natural beauty, softly coiffed hair, tender smile, and heart of gold made her my all-time favorite teacher. Her memory still rests with me today.

Mrs. Coleman was the first teacher who permitted me to "work" in her classroom. I was at "work" when I helped my peers understand concepts and when I sorted, stapled, or graded papers. My world was open to so many possibilities, and I embraced them all. It was then, at age eight, that I declared my lifelong career choice as a teacher. And, I was so very dedicated and determined to be an educator. I did not wait until I graduated college. I started right then.

The summer after third grade, I assisted Mrs. Coleman with cleaning out her file cabinets, etc. She wanted to clear out old worksheets and replace them with updated material. I intervened when she was about to throw the papers into the trash bin. I couldn't imagine all of that good paper being tossed away and wasted. I told her I would take them. And, that is exactly what I did. I took all, and I mean all, the worksheets home. My mother was shocked, to say the least, when I walked to the car with two armloads of papers.

Once I returned home with my stacks and stacks of merchandise, I organized them by subjects and themes. Most of the worksheets I completed myself for extra practice, and the other worksheets were given to my "students." My students consisted of my brothers and my cousins (when they would come to visit). Did my students enjoy playing school with me? I'm sure they did not, but it was always my primary game of choice. Most of the time, I forced them to play. But, I have no regrets or apologies for my behavior. It made me an excellent educator and them better students!

After the experiences of preschool/kindergarten to third grade, educationally and professionally my choices and my future were set. The Lord provided many opportunities for me to prepare for all that lay ahead for me. There is nothing I regret in any of it. To God be the glory!

Next are a few examples from the Bible to demonstrate how God prepared others in their youth for the mantle they would carry when the time came to walk fully in their calling.

First up is Joseph. Joseph was a dreamer himself, but he also had the gift of interpretation. This gift ushered him into many high positions of authority. Specifically, the gift granted him access into Pharaoh's kingdom, giving him the seat of second in command. He had experienced difficulties along the way, but God was with him and guided him right where he was predestined.

Read Genesis 37:5-8 (NIV). *"Joseph had a dream, and when he told it to his brothers, they hated him all the more. He said to them, 'Listen to this dream I had: We were binding sheaves of grain out in the field when suddenly my sheaf rose and stood upright, while your sheaves gathered around mine and bowed down to it.' His brothers said to him, 'Do you intend to reign over us? Will you actually rule us?' And they hated him all the more because of his dream and what he had said."*

Notice this- people will develop a hatred for you when you strive to seek after your dreams and for merely sharing your dreams with them. Sometimes, instead of encouraging you to succeed, they try to discourage you or thwart your success.

Now, read Genesis 39:20-40:23 (NIV). *"Joseph's master took him and put him in prison, the place where the king's prisoners were confined. But while Joseph was there in the prison, the Lord was with him; he showed him kindness and granted him favor in the eyes of the prison warden. So the warden put Joseph in charge of all those held in the prison, and he was made responsible for all that was done there. The warden paid no attention to anything under Joseph's care, because the Lord was with Joseph and gave him success in whatever he did. Some time later, the cupbearer and the baker of the king of Egypt offended their master, the king of Egypt. Pharaoh was angry with his two officials, the chief cupbearer and the chief baker, and put them in custody in the house of the captain of the guard, in the same prison where Joseph was confined. The captain of the guard assigned them to Joseph, and he attended them. After they had been in custody for some time, each of the two men—the cupbearer and the baker of the king of Egypt, who were being held in prison—had a dream the same night, and each dream had a meaning of its own.*

When Joseph came to them the next morning, he saw that they were dejected. So he asked Pharaoh's officials who were in custody with him in his master's house, 'Why do you look so sad today?' 'We both had dreams,' they answered, 'but there is no one to interpret them.' Then Joseph said to them, 'Do not interpretations belong to God? Tell me your dreams.' So the chief cupbearer told Joseph his dream. He said to him, 'In my dream I saw a vine in front of me, and on the vine were three branches. As soon as it budded, it blossomed, and its clusters ripened into grapes. Pharaoh's cup was in my hand, and I took the grapes, squeezed them into Pharaoh's cup and put the cup in his hand.' 'This is what it means,' Joseph said to him. 'The three branches are three days. Within three days Pharaoh will lift up your head and restore you to your position, and you will put Pharaoh's cup in his hand, just as you used to do when you were his cupbearer. But when all goes well with you, remember me and show me kindness; mention me to Pharaoh and get me out of this prison. I was forcibly carried off from the land of the Hebrews, and even here I have done nothing to deserve being put in a dungeon.' When the chief baker saw that Joseph had given a favorable interpretation, he said to Joseph, 'I too had a dream: On my head were three baskets of bread. In the top basket were all kinds of baked goods for Pharaoh, but the birds were eating them out of the basket on my head.' 'This is what it means,' Joseph said. 'The three baskets are three days. Within three days Pharaoh will lift off your head and impale your body on a pole. And the birds will eat away your flesh.' Now the third day was Pharaoh's birthday, and he gave a feast for all his officials. He lifted up the heads of the chief cupbearer and the chief baker in the presence of his officials: He restored the chief cupbearer to his position, so that he once again put the cup into Pharaoh's hand- but he impaled the chief baker, just as Joseph had said to them in his interpretation. The chief cupbearer, however, did not remember Joseph; he forgot him."

God has the final say and regardless of the wicked heart of men, God's heart remains pure, and His justice reigns supreme.

Read Genesis 41:1-43 (NIV). *"When two full years had passed, Pharaoh had a dream: He was standing by the Nile, when out of the river there came up seven cows, sleek and fat, and they grazed among the reeds. After them, seven other cows, ugly and gaunt, came up out of the Nile and stood beside those on the riverbank. And the cows that were ugly and gaunt ate up the seven sleek, fat cows. Then Pharaoh woke up. He fell asleep again and had a second dream: Seven heads of grain, healthy and good, were growing on a single stalk. After them, seven other heads of grain sprouted—thin and scorched by the east wind. The thin heads of grain swallowed up the seven healthy, full heads. Then Pharaoh woke up; it had been a dream. In the morning his mind was troubled, so he sent for all the magicians and wise men of Egypt. Pharaoh told them his dreams, but no one could interpret them for him. Then the chief cupbearer said to Pharaoh, 'Today I am reminded of my shortcomings. Pharaoh was once angry with his servants, and he imprisoned me and the chief baker in the house of the captain of the guard. Each of us had a dream the same night, and each dream had a meaning of its own. Now a young Hebrew was there with us, a servant of the captain of the guard. We told him our dreams, and he interpreted them for us, giving each man the interpretation of his dream. And things turned out exactly as he interpreted them to us: I was restored to my position, and the other man was impaled.' So Pharaoh sent for Joseph, and he was quickly brought from the dungeon. When he had shaved and changed his clothes, he came before Pharaoh. Pharaoh said to Joseph, "I had a dream, and no one can interpret it. But I have heard it said of you that when you hear a dream you can interpret it.' 'I cannot do it,' Joseph replied to Pharaoh, 'but God will give Pharaoh the answer he desires.' Then Pharaoh said to Joseph, 'In my dream I was standing on the bank of the Nile, when out of the river there came up seven cows, fat and sleek, and they grazed among the reeds. After them, seven other cows came up—scrawny and very ugly and lean. I had never seen such ugly cows in all the land of Egypt. The lean, ugly cows ate up the seven fat cows that came up first. But even after they ate them, no one could tell that they had done so; they looked just as ugly as before. Then I woke up.'In my dream I saw seven heads of grain, full and good, growing on a single stalk. After them, seven other heads sprouted—withered and thin and scorched by the east wind. The thin heads of grain swallowed up the seven good heads. I told this to the magicians, but none of them could explain it to me.' Then Joseph said to Pharaoh, 'The dreams of Pharaoh are one and the same. God has revealed to Pharaoh what he is about to do. The seven good cows are seven years, and the seven good heads of grain are seven years; it is one and the same dream. The seven lean, ugly cows that came up afterward are seven years, and so are the seven worthless heads of grain scorched by the east wind: They are seven years of famine. 'It is just as I said to Pharaoh: God has shown Pharaoh what he is about to do. Seven years of great abundance are coming throughout the land of Egypt, but seven years of famine will follow them. Then all the abundance in Egypt will be forgotten, and the famine will ravage the land. The abundance in the land will not be remembered, because the famine that follows it will be so severe. The reason the dream was given to Pharaoh in two forms is that the matter has been firmly decided by God, and God will do it soon. 'And now let Pharaoh look for a discerning and wise man and put him in charge of the land of Egypt. Let Pharaoh appoint commissioners over the land to take a fifth of the harvest of Egypt during the seven years of abundance. They should collect all the food of these good years that are coming and store up the grain under the authority of*

Pharaoh, to be kept in the cities for food. This food should be held in reserve for the country, to be used during the seven years of famine that will come upon Egypt, so that the country may not be ruined by the famine.' The plan seemed good to Pharaoh and to all his officials. So Pharaoh asked them, 'Can we find anyone like this man, one in whom is the spirit of God?' Then Pharaoh said to Joseph, 'Since God has made all this known to you, there is no one so discerning and wise as you. You shall be in charge of my palace, and all my people are to submit to your orders. Only with respect to the throne will I be greater than you.' So Pharaoh said to Joseph, 'I hereby put you in charge of the whole land of Egypt.' Then Pharaoh took his signet ring from his finger and put it on Joseph's finger. He dressed him in robes of fine linen and put a gold chain around his neck. He had him ride in a chariot as his second-in-command, and people shouted before him, 'Make way!' Thus he put him in charge of the whole land of Egypt."

Although at times you may feel discouraged and believe your dream is delayed, God has not forgotten you. He is working behind the scene, and His timing is always perfect.

Jeremiah was another one of God's servants who started as a lad. He questioned his own calling because of his age or lack of experience. Read Jeremiah 1:4-7. *"The word of the Lord came to me, saying, 'Before I formed you in the womb I knew you, before you were born I set you apart; I appointed you as a prophet to the nations.' 'Alas, Sovereign Lord,' I said, 'I do not know how to speak; I am too young.' But the Lord said to me, "Do not say, 'I am too young.' You must go to everyone I send you to and say whatever I command you. Do not be afraid of them, for I am with you and will rescue you,' declares the Lord. Then the Lord reached out his hand and touched my mouth and said to me, 'I have put my words in your mouth. See, today I appoint you over nations and kingdoms to uproot and tear down, to destroy and overthrow, to build and to plant.'"*

We must learn to see ourselves the way God sees us and for the purpose for which He created us. We, along with others, can deceive ourselves, believing we are incapable of completing specific tasks. However, it would be to our benefit to align our thoughts with those of the Creator.

Jesus, the Son of God, came to Earth as a servant. Although He is the second person in the triune godhead, He came to fulfill a specific role in the earth.

Luke 2:41-52 (NIV) says, *"Every year Jesus' parents went to Jerusalem for the Festival of the Passover. When he was twelve years old, they went up to the festival, according to the custom. After the festival was over, while his parents were returning home, the boy Jesus stayed behind in Jerusalem, but they were unaware of it. Thinking he was in their company, they traveled on for a day. Then they began looking for him among their relatives and friends. When they did not find him, they went back to Jerusalem to look for him. After three days they found him in the temple courts, sitting among the teachers, listening to them and asking them questions. Everyone who heard him was amazed at his understanding and his answers. When his parents saw him, they were astonished. His mother said to him, 'Son, why have you treated us like this? Your father and I have been anxiously searching for you.' 'Why were you searching for me?' he asked. 'Didn't you know I had to be in my Father's house?' But they did not understand what he was saying to them. Then he went down to Nazareth with them and was obedient to them. But his mother treasured all these things in her heart. And Jesus grew in wisdom and stature, and in favor with God and man."*

This passage is the first recording of Jesus' words. And what powerful words they are. He is demonstrating He is about His father's business, which He later emphasizes when He says, *"For I have come down from heaven not to do my will but to do the will of him who sent me"* (John 6:38, NIV).

Wisdom will lead us to fulfill our God-given calling and not our own will. Our life will be much more fruitful if we align our will with God's. For a deeper understanding of the scripture, read Matthew Henry's Concise Commentary on Luke 2:41-52:

> It is for the honour of Christ that children should attend on public worship. His parents did not return till they had stayed all the seven days of the feast. It is well to stay to the end of an ordinance, as becomes those who say, It is good to be here. Those that have lost their comforts in Christ, and the evidences of their having a part in him, must bethink themselves where, and when, and how they lost them, and must turn back again. Those that would recover their lost acquaintance with Christ, must go to the

place in which he has put his name; there they may hope to meet him. They found him in some part of the temple, where the doctors of the law kept their schools; he was sitting there, hearkening to their instructions, proposing questions, and answering inquiries, with such wisdom, that those who heard were delighted with him. Young persons should seek the knowledge of Divine truth, attend the ministry of the gospel, and ask such questions of their elders and teachers as may tend to increase their knowledge. Those who seek Christ in sorrow, shall find him with the greater joy. Know ye not that I ought to be in my Father's house; at my Father's work; I must be about my Father's business. Herein is an example; for it becomes the children of God, in conformity to Christ, to attend their heavenly Father's business, and make all other concerns give way to it. Though he was the Son of God, yet he was subject to his earthly parents; how then will the foolish and weak sons of men answer it, who are disobedient to their parents? However we may neglect men's sayings, because they are obscure, yet we must not think so of God's sayings. That which at first is dark, may afterwards become plain and easy. The greatest and wisest, those most eminent, may learn of this admirable and Divine Child, that it is the truest greatness of soul to know our own place and office; to deny ourselves amusements and pleasures not consistent with our state and calling.

Ugly Duckling Phase

ACT II

The one bird who did not, could not,

Fit in

My mother and brothers laughed

At me

I feel like I do not belong in here

In this place

I am a small black pea

In a sea of white grains

No time or place

Cast Out

Ostracized

Isolated

Different

From my family

Until I learned

I am not an ugly duckling

Not a deformed bird

But a

Beautiful

Gorgeous

Stunning

Swan

By Nick Oldberg

Most people have heard the analogy of the ugly duckling, which was derived from the book *The Ugly Duckling* by Danish poet and author Hans Christian Andersen. The story shares the account of a plain-looking, homely duck that was born in a barnyard. At the hands of his brothers, sisters, and others in the barnyard, the duck suffered much physical, verbal, and emotional abuse. Sadly, he wandered from the barnyard and lived with wild ducks and geese until a hunter slaughtered the flock. From there, the duck attempted to secure shelter elsewhere. First, he saw a flock of migrating wild swans. But, because he could not fly, it was a hopeless desire to attempt to join them. Next, the duck came upon a farmer and lodged with him.

Due to unforeseen circumstances, the duck's stay with the farmer was short. Eventually, the duck found himself alone and cold. But, time continued to move forward, and the duck matured, becoming full grown. Spring arrived, and the duck came across a group of swans. At that point in his existence, he was unable to further endure a life of solitude and hardship and decided it would be better to be killed by such beautiful birds than to live a life of ugliness and misery. To his surprise, the swans welcomed and accepted him. By chance, the duck looked into the water, seeing his reflection, and realized he had physically matured into one of them. He and his new family took flight and soared into the air.

The moral of the story is a powerful message about self-esteem and acceptance as well as the importance of kindness to others, a concept derived from Scripture, namely Matthew 7:12 (known as The Golden Rule), which states, *"Therefore all things whatsoever ye would that men should do to you, do ye even so to them: for this is the law and the prophets"* (also found in Luke 6:31) and I Corinthians 13:13, which states, *"And now these three remain: faith, hope and love. But the greatest of these is love"* (NIV).

With the prevalence of bullying and now cyber bullying, self-image and kindness are topics that constantly and consistently require the attention of parents and other persons of authority. Without constant and consistent attention to the development of a healthy self-esteem within youth, instances of the ugly duckling syndrome will continue to erode our society.

For most people, their initial self-image is formed as a result of what others think and say about and to them. The thoughts and perceptions of other people tend to become the thoughts and perceptions of the individual. If a person hears negativity on a regular basis, he or she could eventually internalize the negative perceptions and begin to walk out the corresponding behaviors in his or her life unless there are enough positive comments and perceptions being deposited into the person's life to combat the negative. Proverbs 23:7a says, *"For as he thinketh in his heart, so is he."* Therefore, we are what we think we are, which is usually a result of what was deposited through words and actions into our spirits and our soulish realm.

As exemplified in Andersen's book, in most cases when the term "ugly duckling" is used, it refers to a person who is physically unattractive. A duckling, however, is simply a young duck, a duck in its immature stage. As the ugly duckling matures, it sheds its unfavorable characteristics as it comes into its own. The second part of the analogy of the ugly duckling is the comparison to a beautiful swan. A swan is a large water bird with a long, flexible neck and typically has an all-white plumage.

The analogy insinuates the transition of the ugly duckling into the beautiful swan, which is more physically attractive as well as more socially acceptable. Although the transition presents a wonderful, lovely end to a heartbreaking fairytale, technically that type of transition is metamorphically impossible because ducklings can only transition into ducks. Nevertheless, the imagery is not lost. Those reading the fairytale understand what is being stated.

You may be wondering how the ugly duckling metaphor fits into my story. Allow me to enlighten you. I went through a transitional period similar to what is being alluded to in the analogy. Yet, my transition was not external; rather, it was a series of internal psychological shifts, which precipitated an outward behavioral transition.

Beginning in the third grade, at age eight, I began to discover and embrace my passions of both learning and then teaching that which I have learned. At the same time, my teachers took notice and began to nurture my innate, God-given abilities. However, some of my peers had thoughts of their own about me and how my teachers responded to me.

On a typical day of school, from grade three through commencement from the sixth grade, my teachers would introduce new concepts to us students or refresh our memories of old concepts. I would readily catch onto the day's concepts and complete the assignment straight away. Meanwhile, in the course of a given day, teachers at the elementary level always had tasks that needed completing, and they often had student volunteers to complete the tasks. These tasks included anything from stapling papers to sorting papers to grading worksheets from provided answer keys.

When I finished the required assignments, my teachers always gave me a task to complete. Otherwise, I would be sitting idly at my desk or perhaps reading a book (as I was a book junkie) because I completed the activities rather quickly. Not only did I read complete novels in record time, but I also read series of novels, back to back to back. If I were not engaged in a task or reading a book, I could be found leaning over someone's desk, instructing him or her on the proper methods needed to complete the activity.

Eventually, my patterns of assisting my peers were noticed by my teachers. Afterward, they began to make an example of me and routinely allowed me to assist my peers. Personally, I did not mind the attention. And, it was never intended to showcase me or set me apart from others. Nevertheless, the attention I received was not readily appreciated by my peers. They disliked the attention I received from our teachers and began to ridicule me as a result and treat me as though I was different from them and not a nine-year-old fourth-grade student in the same class.

Children, as well as many immature adults, take issue with what they perceive to be preferential treatment toward someone of like kind. They believe each person in a given context must be treated equally, unless the person suffers from an abnormality, such as an obvious mental or physical disablement.

Let us examine that mindset for a moment to understand the reality and depth of equal treatment. To treat individuals equally means to treat them in the same manner in an effort to be fair. In a scenario where two students who are in the same class and are completing a math assignment, Student A is familiar with the material, and Student B is not. They both receive the same amount of instruction and assistance in completing the assignment. That would be a demonstration of equality. Sounds good? Well, what if I further explained that at the end of the lesson, Student A earned a score of 90%, while Student B earned only 74%. How would you view equal treatment then?

Most people could easily offer an explanation for the grade disparity. Some would say Student A is stronger in math. Others would argue Student B doesn't have good study habits. The list of reasons could go on and on; however, the explanation could have more to do with the equal instruction they received with no regard to their past. So, let's go a step further.

The converse of equality is equity. While equality focuses on fairness through the distribution of equal treatment, equity takes into consideration an individual's starting position. If Student A was familiar with the material contained within the math assignment or was stronger in math, he or she had an advantage and, as a result, scored higher. However, if the teacher witnessed Student B struggling with the assignment and discerned his or her lack of understanding the concepts, the teacher could have provided additional assistance or sent the student to a tutor. If the tutoring sessions were successful, then Student B would be in a position to earn a higher grade due to a higher level of understanding. That is an example of equitable treatment, giving an individual what he or she needs to be successful. Obviously, Student A did not need additional assistance. However, Student B could have benefited from tutoring. Having viewed the scenario in light of both viewpoints, which would you consider the best approach-equality or equity?

In my situation, my teachers did what they believed was best for the situation. Exercising equity, they nurtured my gifts while at the same time getting the assistance they needed in completing classroom tasks and also giving other students additional assistance by having me function as an in-class tutor. It was not done to the neglect or detriment of another student's learning. However, due to the lack of understanding on the part of my peers, their continued attitude toward me, as well as labeling me as the teacher's pet, my introvert qualities rose to the surface, causing me to elect to not engage with my peers on a regular basis outside the classroom. I actually felt more comfortable being alone in my self-created shell or with my teachers. During recess, I would stay inside the classroom, and during the lunch hour, after I ate, I would return to the classroom to assist my teachers. At first, my teachers when encourage me to go out, but I would flat out refuse. Eventually, each teacher came to know my pattern and expected to see me during those times of day. That was my pattern from grades four to six.

In a sense, I retreated just as the ugly duckling had. He was not accepted by his family and peers because of his looks. Similarly, I was not accepted because of the perceived preferential treatment I received. In all fairness, I must say- not all of my classmates were unkind; there were only a select few. Most of the others probably could have cared less about the entire situation. However, regardless of the actual number of students who opposed me, there were enough to alter my behavior at that time in my life. Later, I will explain my personality make-up, which coupled with this situation helped to form the shell that served as my protection.

When people find comfort in a particular environment, they have a tendency to gravitate toward the familiar territory, which has commonly become known as the comfort zone. According to Judith Bardwick (1995), author of *Danger in the Comfort Zone*, the comfort zone is a behavioral state where a person operates in an anxiety-neutral position. Brené Brown, a research professor at the University of Houston, describes a comfort zone as "where our uncertainty, scarcity and vulnerability are minimized - where we believe we will have access to enough love, food, talent, time, and admiration. Where we feel we have some control" (quoted in Tugend, 2011, *Tiptoeing out of One's Comfort Zone*). The need for a comfort zone certainly played out in my life.

Once I matriculated from elementary school at age eleven, my next stage was the junior high school platform. The uncharted experience of seventh grade was exciting, going from one class to the next, etc., etc. Although I met many new people, the crowds of people were a bit overwhelming for the introverted extrovert that I was and still am. I found I was more comfortable in my old habitat of Broadacres Elementary School. Furthermore, I had grown very accustomed to assisting others with their learning, and those opportunities were not as readily available as they had previously been. Moreover, my present teachers frowned upon students conversing unnecessarily during class time. Therefore, I was left with only one option to fulfill my desires of assisting others in their learning process: I had to return to the scene where my desire had been birthed. So, my journey began.

Somehow, and I do not recall exactly how, I was able to leave the junior high campus (probably after fifth period or lunch) and go to my alma mater: Broadacres Elementary School, to serve as a tutor, while earning course credit. Taking the walk from Curtis Junior High each afternoon was the highlight of my day. I don't know how I was able to convince my very protective mother to allow me to walk from one campus to the other, but she agreed. And for that, I was grateful. Upon my arrival at Broadacres, I would check in at the front office and then proceed to my assigned classroom. Typically, I worked with students in what was deemed as the upper grades (fourth through sixth). Assisting the students with their assignments or grading papers fortified my strengths in all subjects across the curriculum. For two years (seventh and eighth grade), that was my routine. By ninth grade though, I had settled into junior high school life at age fourteen and transitioned into high school after commencement.

For the three years of high school, I focused on preparing for college by taking all college preparatory courses. After my experiences with tutoring and interacting with teachers, I was certain that my career choice was unmistakable, so I knew college was in my future, as a bachelor's degree was and still is required to teach students in the K-12 educational system in the state of California.

Now, let's examine how and when I came out of my shell, a shell I had constructed after suffering through my peers' ridicule, as a method of both escape and protection. The first successful attempt at demolishing the barricade I had built occurred when I was yet in junior high school as I consistently made my journey to the elementary school campus. Each day, I traversed the same path, navigating from point A to point B, I grew increasingly confident and comfortable with myself as an apprentice educator, causing the strength of the walls around me to weaken. The younger students enjoyed having my assistance, and the teachers showed me respect as I gave them all my attention, so I could glean from their several abilities.

Subsequently, during the summer between junior and senior high, I engaged in my first summer job, which was at a daycare center. Although the job was designed to only last two months or so, each day when I went to the center, I was overjoyed to work with the toddlers and to assist the teachers with any tasks they needed to accomplish. During that summer, I learned plenty about caring for young children just as I had acquired an abundance of information during my volunteer service on the elementary campus, such as how to effectively deliver information in a comprehensible manner, so hungry minds could partake of it. My interactions with the preschool staff as well as the young children were proof positive that my abilities could impact someone's life and that was a gifting of which I could be proud. In those two and a half months, the fortress I had built around me began to fade further into the background.

Thereafter, in high school, I, along with my peers, was constantly being asked by teachers and counselors alike about my career objective. After answering "teacher" repeatedly, my choice was completely and permanently embedded in my psyche. Furthermore, family members and friends of the family also inquired about my plans after high school. Answering all of the inquiries and subsequent questions boosted my confidence as well because I was certain I would be a great teacher – even at an early age. I was doubtless about my ability to comprehend information and then disseminate it to willing, open minds.

Sometime after graduating high school, my shell continued to erode, as I grew increasingly comfortable with myself and the career path onto which I would soon be headed.

Finally, the positive feedback I received from teachers, peers, parents, and family assisted in laying a sturdy foundation of self-esteem, causing my outer fortress to completely erode. To the credit of my mother, grandmother, and other family, I always had familial support. Actually, most of the people who have been prevalent in my life have been positive influences. The entire fiasco with my fourth-grade experience demonstrates how both positive and negative forces/comments/attitude/behaviors can impact a person's life. Unfortunately, sometimes people fail to understand the impact their words and actions can have in altering another person's course. Therefore, it is imperative that we are careful about what we say and do. We can never effectively assess another's fragility. At the same time, it is equally important for an individual to know who he or she is, even when he or she is a child. This knowledge can potentially prevent one's course from being altered or at least drastically altered.

Ironically, as God would have it, as I was in the midst of composing this chapter, on a Saturday afternoon in February, I attended the annual Founders' Day program for my sorority. The keynote speaker was a beautiful, intelligent, and articulate woman: Dr. Lucretia Taylor, who is an associate program director for teens and young adults. After dancing to the podium to her theme song for the day, she began to craftily and artfully share a synoptic version of her biography. In her rendition, there was a portion that fully captured my attention, as it mirrored an experience I shared with you only a few pages ago. Dr. Taylor said, "When I was in fourth grade, excelling in my studies and being on the honor roll, at nine years old, the other girls did not like me. So, I felt more comfortable staying inside during recess and lunch. I would help my teacher with whatever I could, such as stapling papers, etc. When the other children teased me, my teacher stopped them and said, 'No, she's a leader'."

Hearing Dr. Taylor's account of her fourth grade year and what she had experienced at the hands and mouths of her peers was enlightening for me. This is what the Holy Spirit revealed to me: Intelligent, overachieving children who stand out from the crowd, who have been separated by God for His purpose, are more times than not misunderstood and underappreciated by their peers. It was heartbreaking to hear Dr. Taylor recount her experiences, but at the same time, I found comfort with the realization I was not alone in my experiences.

To further demonstrate how a person can be misunderstood and then isolated from his/her own family, peers, or society at large, read the following biblical accounts.

First, according to Genesis Chapters 37-50, Joseph, the eleventh son of the Israelite patriarch Jacob, at the age of seventeen, was marginalized by ten of his brothers. However, the separation process had already begun years before, not long after Joseph's birth. When Joseph was born, it can be surmised by the supplied facts that Jacob was overjoyed to finally have his barren wife Rachel give birth to their first child. Jacob loved Rachel deeply and had desired to marry her for many years prior to their nuptials actually taking place.

Here is the backstory to Jacob and Rachel's marriage. Jacob had asked Rachel's father Laban for her hand in marriage and made the proper arrangements to work for Laban for seven years. After completing the seven years, wedding vows were exchanged. However, on the morning after the long-awaited wedding night, Jacob discovered he had been duped. He opened his eyes to learn his bride was Leah, Rachel's older and less attractive sister. However, after much discussion and the weeklong wedding celebrations came to an end, Jacob took Rachel as his wife also, with her father's permission.

Then, the time came for the wives to bear children, but only Leah conceived. Rachel was only able to bear children for her husband through her handmaiden, who was her younger sister. Although Leah bore sons for Jacob, she too offered her handmaiden (another younger sister) to him through which to bear additional sons. Finally, as stated earlier, after Jacob had ten sons (and one daughter) with none coming from Rachel's womb, God, in all His majesty, heard Rachel's plea and opened her womb, allowing her to conceive. She brought forth a son, whom Jacob named Joseph.

Any onlooker would have thought Joseph was the firstborn son because from that moment forward, Jacob loved Joseph the most of all his sons because he was the son of Jacob's old age and he was Rachel's son. Later, Rachel conceived another son, and as she lay there taking her final breath, she named him Ben-Oni, meaning "son of my sorrow" because childbirth had literally caused the life to drain from her. After his wife's passing, Jacob changed his son's name to Benjamin, meaning "son of my right hand."

Due to the favoritism Joseph found with his father, his ten older brothers greatly despised him. At age seventeen, Joseph would report to Jacob any wrongdoings his brothers committed. That, of course, did not fare well with them at all. Then, when Joseph began to dream and share his dreams with his brothers, he was further marginalized, as his dreams seemed to depict Joseph as being superior to his brothers.

As a result of the ill feelings and infuriation the ten brothers felt towards Joseph, they orchestrated a plot to cause his demise. Most of them wanted to shed his blood; however, the oldest brother Ruben spoke up and literally saved Joseph's life. Instead, Joseph was thrown into a pit after the coat of many colors his father had made for him was stripped from his body. Joseph was pulled from the pit and sold into slavery to the Ishmaelites.

From there, Joseph was sold again to Potiphar who later had him thrown in jail as a result of a false accusation uttered by Potiphar's wife. After all the trials and tribulations, Joseph eventually found himself second in command to Pharaoh over the entire land of Egypt. Then, a famine hit Canaan, the land in which his family resided. Due to the famine, Jacob sent two of his sons to Egypt to seek food staples, with the understanding Egypt was in great supply. It was then that Joseph was reconnected with his family although at the initial meeting his brothers were unaware of his identity, for sixteen years had passed. He was no longer the teenage boy whose demise they had attempted to construct.

To bring the story to a close, God had allowed for the mistreatment of Joseph at the hands and mouths of his very own flesh and blood: his brothers. Although they had different mothers, they all had their father's blood flowing through their veins. Joseph's brothers had counted him out. To them, he was an unwanted and unnecessary source of agitation, and they believed they could take matters into their own hands to expurgate him from their lives.

The one important factor they had the neglected to take into consideration was the Almighty God. He, who is the author and finisher of our faith, was writing Joseph's story, and He had a purpose for Joseph's life. All of the hardships Joseph endured were strategically orchestrated by God in order to place him in a position of power in the land of Egypt, so the Israelites could find favor when the famine hit Canaan. After all, God had promised Jacob's grandfather Abraham, he would be a father of many nations.

After Joseph revealed his identity to his brothers, eventually his entire family took residence in Egypt. All seventy of them were welcomed by Pharaoh due to his relationship with Joseph. Later, the Israelites multiplied in number and still exist today. Without God's hand upon Joseph's life, orchestrating his course, the Israelites could have very well expired in Canaan during the famine, with exception to Joseph and his two sons: Manasseh and Ephraim, who were in Egypt.

The second account of segregation or discounting one's value is of Israel's second king: David. In the book of I Samuel Chapter 16, the details of David being anointed as king of Israel are provided. But first, let's review the events, which are recorded in I Samuel Chapter 15.

Saul had previously been anointed as king by Samuel after the Israelites had requested of God an earthly king. However, during the course of Saul's reign, God gave him specific instructions to be carried out. For example, when going into battle with the Amalekites, God told Saul the Amalekites were to be completely annihilated and all that belonged to them, being careful not to spare anyone or anything. However, after the Israelite army defeated the Amalekites in battle and killed all of them, Saul spared King Agag's life. That was a direct violation of what God had instructed. To make matters worse, Saul also spared the best sheep and cattle, taking them as his own.

God was furious at Saul's disobedience and declared in verse 11, *"It repenteth me that I have set up Saul to be king: for he is turned back from following me, and hath not performed my commandments. And it grieved Samuel; and he cried unto the LORD all night."* Although Samuel had to deliver the message to Saul regarding God's new plan, he too was disappointed in the recent chain of events. God, on the other hand, was ready to move on and replace Saul, so He asked Samuel, *"How long wilt thou mourn for Saul, seeing I have rejected him from reigning over Israel? fill thine horn with oil, and go, I will send thee to Jesse the Bethlehemite: for I have provided me a king among his sons"* (Ch. 16, v. 1).

Next, Samuel informed Saul that God had removed His anointing from him and would give it to another, so he could effectively rule Israel. Although Saul was grievously disappointed and sorrowful as a result of God's decision, he only had himself to blame. Then, to compound matters, Samuel rebuked Saul by saying, *"Behold, to obey is better than sacrifice, and to hearken than the fat of rams"* (verse 22b).

Then, God sent Samuel to Bethlehem to anoint the new king, telling him the new king would be one of Jesse's sons. So, Samuel began to make his journey. When he arrived at his destination, he was greeted by elders who were very surprised to see him as they had not been pre-warned of his coming. After speaking with them, he sought out Jesse and his sons and invited them to a sacrifice. Then, before enjoying a meal, there was the assignment Samuel had to complete: anointing the new king.

Upon reviewing the first son Eliab, Samuel surmised by Eliab's stature that he was the one to be anointed, but God said no. That same procedure of surveying each son and thinking he was the one to be anointed continued into all seven sons had been surveyed. God said no to each one. Finally, Samuel asked Jessie if he had any other sons. Jesse acknowledged that he indeed had another son, specifically his youngest son who was presently tending the sheep.

Let us pause for a moment of reflection, by reviewing the facts that have been presented. Samuel, the prophet, arrived in Bethlehem without warning and was greeted by the town's elders, who demonstrated a great concern about his presence. They promptly asked Saul if he had come in peace. Samuel assured them he had and stated he had come for the purpose of a sacrifice. Once he had quelled the elders' concern, Samuel invited Jesse and his sons to the sacrifice. This next bit of information is an important piece of the puzzle, or at the very least, it is interesting.

God had told Samuel one of Jesse's sons would be anointed as the next king of Israel. However, God did not give Samuel the name of the son nor did God tell Samuel how many sons Jesse had. On the other hand, when Jesse and his sons were invited to the sacrifice, neither Jesse nor any of the seven sons who were present considered notifying the absentee son to come along. At that moment and perhaps earlier in his life, the youngest son had been rendered unimportant or at least less important than his brothers. However, their actions could never negate how vitally important he was to God. It was already pre-ordained and pre-destined by God that the young man would play a vital role in Israel's foundation and history.

Let's resume the account to witness the end result. After Jessie confirmed he had one other son, Samuel told him to call in the boy, whose name was David. Upon David's arrival, God said, *"Arise, anoint him: for this is he"* (verse 12b). That was done in the presence of David's father and seven brothers. Can you imagine the astonishment they must have experienced and perhaps the embarrassment? There is a lesson here for all of us.

We should never discount anyone at any time for any task. As humans, we have a tendency to judge from the outward appearance by those attributes that can be readily detected by the eyes. However, God looks not on one's countenance. Rather, He looks at the heart of man along with the gifts and talents He has bestowed within him/her.

After David had been anointed three times and seven years had passed, both King Saul and his son Jonathan were killed in battle. Then, David graced the throne and served as Israel's second king. Who knew he could go from being a shepherd boy to one mighty in battle (defeating the giant Goliath single-handedly) to becoming the king of a great nation? God knew because He and He alone is the divine creator. Hence, we should strive to view people from God's perspective rather than a limited scope that is oftentimes filled with prejudgments rather than wisdom. Seeing people as God does will decrease and possibly eliminate marginalization, separation, isolation, bullying, etc. etc.

The third account of discrimination and separation is found in John 4:1-40 - the story of the Samaritan woman. Being a Samaritan, in and of itself was not viewed in a positive light by the full-blood Jews. Samaritans were half breeds, being half-Jew and half-Gentile, specifically of Assyrian descent.

When Assyria captured the northern kingdom of Israel in 721 BC, some Jews were taken into captivity and transported to Assyria, while others were left behind in their homeland with other Assyrians, who had invaded and taken over the land of Israel. Jews who are left behind in Israel eventually intermarried with Assyrians. The new generation and new race of mixed heritage came to be called Samaritans. And although they have Jewish blood coursing through their veins, Jews do not accept them as their own. So, the Samaritan woman was born with two strikes against her: one was being female, because women at that time and in that culture held low status; the other strike was being a Samaritan, as explained earlier. However, the plot thickens. At the time during her life when she encountered Jesus in the flesh, there were additional stigmas, which further isolated her from society. Here is a summation of her story.

As Jesus and the disciples traveled from Judaea to Gallilee, Jesus made a conscious decision to travel through Samaria rather than traverse around the city as other Jews practiced. In the course of the journey, Jesus grew weary. Upon approaching Jacob's well, Jesus viewed it as a perfect place to take a moment of rest. Not long afterwards, a Samaritan woman, who needed to draw water, approached the well. Jesus, knowing her intentions and finding himself thirsty but lacking the proper instrument with which to draw water, requested from her a drink.

Jesus' request most certainly caught the Samaritan woman off guard as she was keenly aware Jews did not intermingle with Samaritans and men did not typically address women in public who were not their wife or daughter. So, she was doubly baffled. After making her queries known, Jesus responded, yet his response was indirect, not specific to her concerns regarding her race or her sex. Instead, he told her if she knew to whom she was speaking, she would have made a request of her own – for living water – thereby rendering her initial concerns secondary.

Unfortunately, in her spiritual immaturity, the woman failed to ascertain or discern Jesus' meaning of 'living water.' Thus, she took his statement in the natural sense. Her lack of understanding precipitated another question. From there, their banter continued. In the midst of their conversation, Jesus asked the woman to call for her husband, which caused the woman to disclose she had no husband. Jesus responded by saying she had had five husbands and the man she was presently entangled with was not her husband.

Of all that was discussed between Jesus and the Samaritan woman, the portion of the conversation regarding her past relationships is most always highlighted. The woman's numerous marriages had placed her into an immoral context by outsiders passing judgment. Her reputation is always placed at the forefront, which causes her to be easily discounted by both men and women alike.

The focus, however, should be on the value Jesus saw in her and the value she has as a person, regardless of the choices she made regarding men/husbands. Jesus found it necessary to stop and speak with the woman, as He knew she was on her way there and that He would have a private moment with her. That is all any of us needs – just one moment with Jesus, and our lives will be forever changed.

At the end of their conversation, the woman went into town, despite what had been rumored about her and despite her apparent isolation from society, and told all who would listen about a man who had disclosed to her all she had ever done. Her testimony was so compelling many followed her back to meet Jesus for themselves.

That was the outcome Jesus had desired. He proclaimed in John 14:6: *"Jesus saith unto him, I am the way, the truth, and the life: no man cometh unto the Father, but by me."* His sole mission in the earth realm was to redeem a lost and dying world back into right standing with God, the Father, for *"he is the propitiation for our sins: and not for ours only, but also for the sins of the whole world"* (I John 2:2).

Please note - anyone who would be bold enough to assist in His endeavor is with whom He wanted to converse. The Samaritan woman was someone Jesus could count on to speak out. Jesus did not permit her unsavory reputation to deter him from engaging with her as many of the town's people had and as many of us today would have. We find ourselves concerned with how people see us, while we treat others with disdain. We do not want a negative reputation cast upon us, especially due to someone else's folly. Therefore, we tend to stay clear of those who have gained a negative reputation. After all, hasn't it been said, "Birds of a feather flock together"?

On the other side of the coin is another question we need to ask ourselves, "What would Jesus do? Would He interact with people of ill repute from the love within His heart? Would He give them the benefit of the doubt? Would He see them as God, the Father, does? Would He believe they could change if in fact the rumors or negative lifestyle is true?" To answer those questions, the answers to the next two will be evident enough. Were all of Jesus' disciples perfect and upright people? What about Mary Magdalene? We must look far beyond people's reputations and love them in spite of. It could be our interaction with them that breaks walls down, setting them free from the stronghold of their past lives. Everyone deserves a second chance and should therefore be able to re-create themselves as they see fit without being concerned about past mistakes or rumors. Doesn't the Bible say we are a new creation in Him? Old things have passed away and all things have become new?

The fourth account is of Saul of Tarsus, who was converted to Paul, the apostle, found in Acts 9. This story is one of the most amazing and highly regarded testimonials of conversion in Christendom. And, Apostle Paul is by far my most favorite person in the Holy Writ (outside of the Holy Trinity). In a detailed narrative, Saul's account follows (excerpt from "From persecutor to Christian: The conversion of St. Paul," D. D. Emmons, osv.org):

Road to Damascus

Saul, which is Paul's given name, was born into a Jewish family in Tarsus (Turkey) around the year A.D. 8; he was also a Roman citizen, a fact that would play a large role later in his life. Schooled as a Pharisee, he was a tentmaker by trade, but was most noted for his hatred of Christians. He believed the teachings of Jesus violated Mosaic Law, causing him to zealously harass and even jail anyone who followed those teachings.

The first scriptural mention of Saul is found in Acts 7:58, as he is a bystander watching his fellow Jews stone St. Stephen to death. An aggressive persecutor of Christians in Jerusalem, Saul sought and received permission from the high priest to proceed to Damascus for the purpose of imprisoning more followers of Christ.

Most Christians know the story of what happened on the Damascus road: the bright light that knocked Saul down, the voice of Jesus, Saul's blindness and immediate response to the calling of Christ. In the manner of the first apostles who, when beckoned by Christ, gave up their lifestyles to follow him, Saul too doesn't hesitate. He said yes. Blinded from his encounter with Jesus, he allowed himself to be led into Damascus where he was baptized, after which he set out to spread the news of Jesus. Paul would repeat the story of his conversion again and again throughout his life, including to the different magistrates and kings who judged his activities.

Impact of his Conversion

Saul's sudden change confused those around him, because he was known as one who hated Christians, who went about seeking them out to eliminate those individuals he genuinely considered as breaking Jewish law. Suddenly, he was transformed from despising the followers of Jesus into fervently espousing the Gospel of that same Jesus. No one could have anticipated this conversion; it is one of the great miracles of mankind.

After his baptism, Saul, who would be called Paul in the thirteenth chapter of Acts, went to the desert of Arabia to pray and contemplate his calling. He then returned to Damascus and into the synagogue, where he attested to the divinity of

Jesus. While he had no Christian training, God infused words in his heart and in his mouth.

The Jews in Damascus would eventually connive against him. The threat grew so severe that other Christians assisted Paul in an escape that included lowering him over the city walls in a basket. This was only the beginning of the threats and attacks on Paul. Henceforth, he was often regarded as a social undesirable, an agitator, and a leader of a dangerous sect.

From Damascus, he traveled to Jerusalem, where his reputation as a persecutor of Christians preceded him, and Christians there were unsure and confounded by his appearance. There, he met and spent time with Peter, becoming even more determined to serve his Savior.

At the Council of Jerusalem, in the year 49, Paul successfully argued against the widespread belief that non-Jews seeking to become Christians would first have to convert to Judaism, which means comply with Mosaic Law, be circumcised and observe all Jewish dietary customs. Because of Paul's persuasion, Christianity would become even more widespread.

Like the most fervent convert, Paul simply couldn't get enough of Christ. With faith and courage inflamed by the Holy Spirit, Paul would spend the rest of his life going from country to country and town to town proclaiming Jesus as the Messiah, organizing and encouraging Christians to be resolute followers of Jesus, and nonbelievers to open their hearts to Christ, repent and be baptized. He would become known as the Apostle of the Gentiles (non-Jews) and his travels, letters and teaching changed the world.

Often in trouble, Paul was confronted, jailed (though angels rescued him), physically abused and repeatedly endangered and harassed for preaching the message he previously attacked. Despite all the dangers he encountered, Paul never faltered or failed his God. In the end, he would be taken to Rome as a prisoner and be beheaded for his teachings.

Why Paul?

Why would Jesus select the likes of Paul? There were certainly other devoted followers of Jesus available in those early days of the Church - followers ready to give their lives to proclaim Jesus Christ as savior of the world. But Jesus picked and converted this Pharisee, known as Saul, saying, "This man is a chosen instrument of mine to carry my name before Gentiles, kings and Israelites" (Acts 9:15). God selected this man who had a strong hatred of all Jesus stands for, a man who went into the houses of Christians and "dragging out men and women," then "handed them over for imprisonment" (Acts 8:3). This man became God's chosen instrument to spread the message of Jesus across the Middle East and parts of Europe. Certainly, our Lord works in mysterious ways.

Like most misfits and those who served as agitators, Paul was perceived as one of the most unlikely candidates to be used as a mouthpiece for God. His previous activities had placed him into that category. It was not a perception someone had falsely constructed of him. Rather, the perception was derived from Paul's own past actions. However, Paul's past could not and did not prevent God from making him into a new creature. What is very interesting is

God used Paul's fire and zeal for His glory! God will take you with your unique personality but shift your mindset to make you fit to serve as His mouthpiece (Romans 12:2).

Finally, we come to the last biblical account I have chosen to share although there are undoubtedly numerous others. Thus far, we witnessed how Joseph, David, the Samaritan woman, and Apostle Paul all experienced isolation, separation, ridicule, prejudgment, and/or bullying in their individual life. Our Lord and Savior Jesus experienced instances of the same during the thirty-three years He spent on earth. So you see, no one is exempt from cruel and inhumane treatment.

Jesus, the Son of Man, was set apart for God's glory, exemplified by His birth by immaculate conception (Matthew 1:18) and the following passage. Luke 2:41-52 (NIV) shares an account of Jesus, at age twelve, leaving His parents to sit among religious teachers in the temple, listening and asking questions. When scolded by His parents of His apparent neglect, He told His mother that He was in His father's house.

Then, when the time came for Jesus to begin His earthly ministry, at age thirty, God's plan for His life did not render Him exempt from tests and trials or subjugated hatred from His enemies. In Matthew 13: 53-58, we see how Jesus was rejected at Nazareth, the place he called home: *"Now it came to pass, when Jesus had finished these parables, that He departed from there. When He had come to His own country, He taught them in their synagogue, so that they were astonished and said, 'Where did this Man get this wisdom and these mighty works? Is this not the carpenter's son? Is not His mother called Mary? And His brothers James, Joses, Simon, and Judas? And His sisters, are they not all with us? Where then did this Man get all these things?' So they were offended at Him. But Jesus said to them, 'A prophet is not without honor except in his own country and in his own house.' Now He did not do many mighty works there because of their unbelief."*

Sometimes due to familiarity, we are rejected by those whom we are closest. Family and friends often fail to see the move of God in our lives. Either they are unwilling to let go of an old relationship or mindset or their vision is clouded by the past. To further compound Jesus' rejection, not only was He ostracized in His hometown, but it continued with those who heard His preaching as He traveled.

There are two places in John where the Jews wanted to kill Jesus with stones. Both of these occur after Jesus spoke and made a claim about Himself. The first was in John 8:58-59, and the second was in John 10:30-33. Here is the context of both verses:

1. John 8:56-59, *"Your father Abraham rejoiced to see My day, and he saw it and was glad." The Jews therefore said to Him, "You are not yet fifty years old, and have You seen Abraham?" Jesus said to them, "Truly, truly, I say to you, before Abraham was born, I am." Therefore they picked up stones to throw at Him; but Jesus hid Himself, and went out of the temple."*
2. John 10:27-36, *"My sheep hear My voice, and I know them, and they follow Me; and I give eternal life to them, and they shall never perish; and no one shall snatch them out of My hand. "My Father, who has*

given them to Me, is greater than all; and no one is able to snatch them out of the Father's hand. "I and the Father are one." The Jews took up stones again to stone Him. Jesus answered them, "I showed you many good works from the Father; for which of them are you stoning Me?" The Jews answered Him, "For a good work we do not stone You, but for blasphemy; and because You, being a man, make Yourself out to be God." Jesus answered them, "Has it not been written in your Law, 'I said, you are gods'? "If he called them gods, to whom the word of God came (and the Scripture cannot be broken), do you say of Him, whom the Father sanctified and sent into the world, 'You are blaspheming,' because I said, 'I am the Son of God'?"

Intermittently, there were some people who believed Jesus to be the Messiah, and they supported His ministry and teachings. Their belief prompted them to share with others. However, some found it difficult to accept Jesus as such. The perfect example is in John 1:45-51: *"Philip findeth Nathanael, and saith unto him, We have found him, of whom Moses in the law, and the prophets, did write, Jesus of Nazareth, the son of Joseph. And Nathanael said unto him, Can there any good thing come out of Nazareth? Philip saith unto him, Come and see. Jesus saw Nathanael coming to him, and saith of him, Behold an Israelite indeed, in whom is no guile! Nathanael saith unto him, Whence knowest thou me? Jesus answered and said unto him, Before that Philip called thee, when thou wast under the fig tree, I saw thee. Nathanael answered and saith unto him, Rabbi, thou art the Son of God;*

thou art the King of Israel. Jesus answered and said unto him, Because I said unto thee, I saw thee under the fig tree, believest thou? thou shalt see greater things than these. And he saith unto him, Verily, verily, I say unto you, Hereafter ye shall see heaven open, and the angels of God ascending and descending upon the Son of man."

Here is Warren Wiersbe's (2007) commentary on the above passage:

> Jesus called Philip personally and Philip trusted and followed Him. We do not know what kind of heart preparation Philip experienced, for usually God prepares a person's heart before He calls him. We do know that Philip proved his faith by seeking to share it with his friend Nathanael. But Nathanael started out a doubter: He did not believe anything worthwhile could come out of Nazareth.
>
> Our Lord was born in Bethlehem, but he grew up in Nazareth and bore that stigma (Matthew 2:19-23). To be called "a Nazarene" (Acts 24:5) meant to be let down on and rejected.
>
> When Nathanael hesitated and argued, Philip adopted our Lord's own words: "Come and see" (John 1:39).
>
> When Nathaniel came to Jesus, he discovered that the Lord already knew all about him. What a shock! By calling him "an Israelite in whom is no guile," Jesus was certainly referring to Jacob, the ancestor of the Jews, a man who used guile to trick his brother, his father, and his father-in-law.
>
> When Jesus revealed his knowledge of Nathanael, where he had been and what he had been doing, that was

enough to convince the man that Jesus was indeed "the Son of God, the King of Israel."

Nevertheless, after ministering to great multitudes and gaining great notoriety, Jesus was still rejected by the masses. The accusations made against Him led to His crucifixion, as the people favored a known insurrectionary to be released rather than Jesus who was innocent of all charges.

Read the account of this injustice in Matthew 27: 26-31, *"Then released he Barabbas unto them: and when he had scourged Jesus, he delivered him to be crucified. Then the soldiers of the governor took Jesus into the common hall, and gathered unto him the whole band of soldiers. And they stripped him, and put on him a scarlet robe. And when they had platted a crown of thorns, they put it upon his head, and a reed in his right hand: and they bowed the knee before him, and mocked him, saying, Hail, King of the Jews! And they spit upon him, and took the reed, and smote him on the head. And after that they had mocked him, they took the robe off from him, and put his own raiment on him, and led him away to crucify him."*

The treatment Jesus suffered was certainly unjust. However, it was part of God's divine plan. Jesus had to be accused, so He could suffer death by crucifixion. It aligns with prophecy that the Messiah, the one without sin, would bear the sins of the world (Isaiah 53:12; Mark 15:27-28).

Having surveyed what would seemingly be the mildest case to the severest, we should have a better understanding of how our lives can be greatly impacted by those nearest us. As you ponder that concept, continue to peruse my account of eradicating the fortress I had constructed.

During my thirties, I spent some time reflecting on my childhood and my childhood experiences as I penned ***Unleashed Anger, Anger Unleashed*** (my fifth book). I recall having a conversation with my mother, asking if I had been shy as a child. In response, she immediately exclaimed, "No," with a hint of absurdity in her tone. Her reasoning was I talked too much to be deemed shy. Despite her shared perspective, I maintain the belief that I was indeed shy as an adolescent although I most certainly was loquacious from an early age. My timidity was another key factor in my retreat.

From my perspective, my makeup is one of an introverted extrovert or an extroverted introvert. Here is my explanation: When I am in the company of individuals with whom I am comfortable, I am able to speak freely around them. Conversely, when I am among strangers and do not have a specific duty to perform (i.e. teach or preach), I tend to locate a vacant seat and quietly place myself into it. My actions continually demonstrate a continued desire for a comfort zone, to either a greater or lesser degree (depending upon the situation).

Nevertheless, along the way of my maturation process from adolescence to teenager to young adult, I became comfortable with who I am and a psychological shift occurred-allowing me to fully accept myself as God intended me to be – one who educates others and does it with strength and grace, while remaining humble.

Afterward, the behavioral shift commenced. Proverbs 23:7a says, *"For as he thinketh in his heart, so is he."* From the time I began to profess I would become a teacher, I began to walk in that role. Many times when someone asks how long I have been teaching, I count from the time I was eight years old, which would be 42 years now. Then, I follow up by giving the actual number of years by saying, "But, I've only been paid for X number of years," which would now be 27 years.

Once I enrolled in college at CSU, San Diego and began my academic journey toward my career objective, I was more confident that one day I would stand in front of the classroom and pour information out to the masses. Each step I made along the journey fortified my resolve. I began to literally walk out my dream. The behavioral shift incited courage and tenacity within me, and I became unstoppable. No one's words or actions could cause me to falter because I had internalized my own words and thoughts rather than those of others – negative or positive. The song "We've Only Just Begun" embodies my perspective, and its lyrics caused me to press toward the mark (Phil. 3:13-14).

I am thankful, grateful, and forever humbled because God made me who He wants me to be: a woman of value, courage, wisdom, intellect, compassion, and integrity. I will forever walk in my calling to serve in an educational capacity to and with anyone who wants to receive, even when others around neglect to understand me or my makeup, for I am uniquely designed. I am uniquely me!

The Alteration

ACT III

In the "Ugly Duckling Phase" chapter, I briefly mentioned circumstances that occurred in my life, causing a great change within me, which subsequently caused a shift in my behavior. Afterward, I mentioned the necessity of undergoing reconditioning at the hands of the Lord: healing and deliverance. This chapter will fully detail what was being alluded to in the previous chapter, as it unfortunately proved to be a vital component in my development, formation, way of life, and train of thought.

At the tender and innocent age of three years old, I lived in Los Angeles in the care of my recently divorced mother, who was then functioning as a single parent of a four-year-old son, a three-year-old daughter, and a one-year-old son. From time to time, my siblings and I would be left in the care of the babysitter when my mother went out for a few hours on a Friday or Saturday night. As a member of the family, the babysitter would relax or sleep in my mother's bedroom until she returned home. On one occasion, I recall being in my mother's bed under the covers with him. Although I do not recall inappropriate touching on that particular occasion, being in bed with an adult male, in and of itself, is questionable. Granted, sometimes children may initiate situations, such as sleeping in an adult's bed while the adult is there. However, it is the responsibility of the adult to deem whether the behavior is appropriate or not.

On one specific occasion, at three or four years of age, I specifically recall "my babysitter" touching me between my legs with a finger or two inside my panties while saying, "Let me see if you are wet. As a young girl, I felt uneasy. I was not in diapers, and I do not recall ever being a bed wetter. Furthermore, I was not prone to wetting myself instead of making it to the little girl's room in a timely manner. So, I was clueless as to why the statement was made, and at the same time, I was bewildered from being touched in that manner. Yes, at three years old, I was actually aware that no one should be touching my vagina.

Although I have no specific recollection of any other incidents involving that particular family member touching me and cannot say for certain that sexual misconduct was taking place, I know I felt violated even at such a young age, which is why the memory stays with me. Consequently, I deemed that incident as my first remembrance of unwanted and unsolicited touching of my genitalia. Although I was young, I knew enough that a man, or any male for that matter, young or old, should not be touching me in such a manner.

It is incidents such as the one described above and the next one I will detail that can awaken the sexual senses of a person before the natural timeframe, which occurs during adolescence as children transition from their pubescent stage into young adulthood. Introducing a child to sex can disrupt the natural course of physical development and mental stability as well, causing one to be sexually stifled or sexually overactive. A child is mentally, physically, and emotionally unable to engage in sexual intercourse or any form of sexual activity. Thus, in the United States, sexual activity of any form that involves a minor has been deemed as sexual abuse and/or sexual assault.

For the sake of clarity, sexual abuse can be hard to define because of the many different forms it can take on, the different levels of frequency, the variation of circumstances it can occur within, and the different relationships that it may be associated with (Hall & Hall, 2001, *The Long-Term Effects of Childhood Sexual Abuse: Counseling implications*). However, Maltz (2002) provides the following definition: "Sexual abuse occurs whenever one person dominates and exploits another by means of sexual activity or suggestion" (Hall & Hall).

Furthermore, Ratican (1992) defines childhood sexual abuse as any sexual act, overt or covert, between a child and an adult (or older child, where the younger child's participation is obtained through seduction or coercion). Additionally, Ratican states irrespective of how childhood sexual abuse is defined, it generally has significant negative and pervasive psychological impacts on its victims (Hall & Hall, 2001).

After the abuse, which could be years later, the victim may show signs of impairment, which may impact his or her personal, intimate, and/or professional life. According to Hall & Hall (2011), "Childhood sexual abuse has been correlated with higher levels of depression, guilt, shame, self-blame, eating disorders, somatic concerns, anxiety, disassociative patterns, repression, denial, sexual problems, and relationship problems."

Another incident of sexual abuse I encountered is aligned most closely with Ratican's definition. I do not recall my exact age at the time of the incident; however, my recollection leads me to say I was between six and eight years of age. Also, to prevent from divulging those directly involved (both innocent and guilty), I have purposefully changed the setting of the offense, the names, and my relationship to the individuals. From my recollection, there were at least five people involved in the incident: an adult male relative, whom I will call Billy; two of his adult male friends, whom I will refer to as Mike and Joe; a young male relative (Bobby), who was approximately a year or two older than I was, and, of course, me.

Here are the details: one afternoon, Bobby and I were visiting Billy, and Mike and Jo stopped by. Billy and his friends were playing around with some tools and knickknacks out in the garage. Bobby and I ventured outside as well. We were curious about what the adults were doing, as it sounded as though they were having a good time. They were young and immature. They were laughing and teasing one another. Then, out of nowhere, one friend thought it would be a good idea to watch two young children have sex. So, they had Bobby and me to remove our pants. Then, they coached Bobby, telling him to insert his penis into me. Thankfully, Bobby was too young to be interested in sex and was sexually inexperienced, so he did not have an erection (not that I knew what an erection was at that time). The lack of an erection prevented penetration. Thank God for that!

For years after the incident, Billy, Mike, and Joe would tease Bobby and me about our attempt at sexual intercourse as if though they had caught us in a planned act of our own rather than one they had maliciously calculated. Fun and games are a natural part of life, but sexual intercourse should never be forced on anyone at any time. Sexual relations should always remain a personal choice.

Unfortunately, the incidences of sexual abuse I encountered throughout my adolescent years are too numerous to detail. However, I will detail two more that impacted my life and my relationships with men.

First, when I was a teenager, I loved spending my weekends and summers with my maternal grandmother. She was my best friend - for my entire life, until she passed on to glory. I could talk to her about any and everything - except the abuse I suffered. I could not and would not tell her about that because I knew it would be heartbreaking for her to hear and know, and I did not want her to hurt for me.

One summer, when I was thirteen years old, I accompanied my grandmother across the street to a neighbor's home. She was going to do a little housework to assist the elderly man because his wife was deathly ill. During the course of her illness, his constant care of her had prevented him from properly cleaning the house for some time.

My grandmother had a kind heart and was always willing to lend a helping hand. She was also a wise woman and knew the mind of a teenager, which is why she took me across the street with her. At that time, I have become infatuated with a teenage boy named Adrian, who was also visiting family for the summer. And, my grandmother knew Adrian was coming around the house often and sitting with me on the back porch, so she informed my mother. Together, my mother and grandmother kept me in check by keeping me in close proximity.

To prevent close contact from occurring between Adrian and me, my grandmother thought it would be best to keep me by her side where she could keep her eyes on me and Adrian's hands off. Unbeknownst to her, by taking me into the neighbor's home, she was actually taking me directly into the lion's den! Danger lay in wait! I would have been safer with Adrian as he was as "green" as I was.

After a few visits to the neighbor's house with my grandmother, the elderly man asked if I could come over and do a little cleaning on the occasions when my grandmother was unable. My grandmother consented. Having gone to his home several times with my grandmother, I had become familiar with him. My familiarity made me comfortable, so I did not mind going over there to do a little housework. After all, my mother and grandmother assured I was well-versed in the art of cleaning. As a young teenager, I do not clean as well as they did, but I definitely knew what needed to be done and how to do it. I even knew which materials and cleansers to use to get the job done.

Upon my arrival to the elderly man's home on my first solo visit, he asked me to wash the dishes and clean the kitchen. He stated my compensation would be a few dollars. I was neither intrigued or impressed by the amount he decided to pay me for cleaning his dirty dishes, but I felt sorry for him and knew he needed my help. Therefore, I readily consented to his list of chores and got right to them without delay.

Furthermore, when I had entered into his home, my nose quickly detected a funny smell. Because I'm very sensitive to smells, I didn't I want to belabor my time there. I desired to complete my chores expediently, so I could physically set myself free. I commenced my short list of chores, looking forward to the child labor wages I would receive. At the age of thirteen, I did not yet have expensive taste or a lavish lifestyle, so a few dollars was all I needed to go to the corner store to purchase my favorite snack: a bottle of Pepsi and a Snickers candy bar. That would cost me all of $.75. I would even have enough money remaining to return to the store the next day to purchase my snack all over again.

Once I had completed cleaning the kitchen, the man placed the money on the counter. I picked up the money and prepared to leave. And to say the least, I was not at all prepared for the next set of words my ears would hear. The elderly man said in a soft, even-toned voice, "I'll give you an extra quarter if you give me a hug." That would be the first time I had ever heard of exchange of money for favors. Frankly, I thought his request was absurd, especially the added part about paying an extra quarter. Why not just ask for a hug?

Nevertheless, as I stated before, I felt sorry for him. I figured he must have felt lonely. After all, his wife was ill, and I had never seen anyone going to visit. So, I leaned in to hug him and received the surprise of a lifetime. When I hugged him, he kissed me. He shoved his old fat wet tongue into my mouth, and at the same time, he grabbed one of my small pubescent breasts and squeezed it. I gagged from the horrible taste of his tongue, which was coated with only God knows what.

In the split second in which the incident occurred, I wondered why he would do such a foul thing to an adolescent, especially with his dying wife lying on her deathbed in the very next room. I was completely perturbed and horrified by what I had just experienced. I choked back my tears, masked my hurt, and left immediately. I ran back across the street to my grandmother's. I never told a soul about how I was humiliated and taken advantage of for a quarter, but I definitely never forgot. As I continued my summer vacation with my loving grandmother, I was careful to stay clear of the old man's home. When I walked to the store, I made sure not to go on his side of the street. And, when my grandmother elected to go over there and clean, I never accompanied her -ever again.

If there was anything I learned from the incident with the old man, it was to stay clear of pedophiles. And that is exactly what I did when I learned who was who. From all my experiences of abuse, I learned a pedophile will show his true colors in any given situation where he believes he can get away with it. Some were even bold enough to try something in a crowded room when everyone's head was turned. Consequently, when a pedophile showed his hand (literally), I made a point to stay clear of him.

The last incident of abuse I will share was different from all others, yet there was one similarity. The one common thread was the perpetrators where are people with whom I was familiar. The difference was, in this case, the offender was very close to my age. In the summer of 1983, just after I had graduated from junior high and was preparing for high school, I spent a lot of time with my best friend whom I will call Linda.

One day, I went from my house to Linda's. From there, we walked across the street to her boyfriend's house. We all stood outside his front door chitchatting for a while. After some time, I noticed a large bulge in his pants. Naïvely, I asked what it was. Obviously, I knew boys/men have a penis. However, at that time, I was a virgin, and I had never seen one erect and would have never imagined one would have been that size. So, when I asked what was in his pants, I thought he had shoved something down there. He and my friend laughed at my question; they probably thought I was teasing. But, in all honesty, I was clueless.

Allow me to digress for a moment. My very protective mother was just that – protective. I led a very sheltered life. I was not able to go any and everyone's house, and no one was allowed past our front door unless they were family. Those were my mother's rules, and my brothers and I had to abide by them. So, quite frankly, I did not know much about sex. At age thirteen, I had never had full on sexual intercourse (which is to be expected), but I had experienced touching as most kids do while playing "house."

On the other hand, my friend Linda had told me plenty about her sexual escapades with her boyfriend and had asked me about mine with Adrian. However, I had nothing to report in that area. Quite frankly, I wasn't yet interested in sex to that degree. It is one thing to play "house" as a youngster, but it's quite another to engage in intercourse. My interest and curiosity began and ended with kissing and what is commonly referred to as light "petting." That was as far as Adrian and I had gone. There was no heavy petting or anything else. Nor was there ever any discussion of going beyond that.

After I kept prodding my friend's boyfriend about what was in his pants, he offered for me to go inside his house, so he could show me. I refused the invitation. He and my friend kept making eye contact with each other, as he continued to invite me inside. I did not understand why I had to go inside to see what was in his pants. I figured he could just take whatever it was out and show me to end the charade. He said if I went with him inside, he would show me. I thought the entire conversation was weird. Then, my friend told me to go on inside because at that point all her boyfriend's attention was on me, and he would not stop asking. Finally, I relented, as I was still curious about the bulge.

Once we were inside, his conversation was completely about sex. He asked me if I had ever had sex before. Maybe, he was starting to figure out how green I was. I didn't want to appear to be a prude – the only one who was inexperienced – so, I said nothing. I left his question unanswered. Even at that point, I still had not put two and two together. I didn't realize the reason he was talking about sex was because the bulge in his pants was his fully erect penis.

Then, my friend's boyfriend asked me if I want to have sex with him. I was really appalled. I told him, "No," as I rolled my eyes at him. He replied, "I think you do." The look in his eyes told me he thought I was playing dumb, and that I knew what he wanted all along. Unfortunately, I was wearing a miniskirt. He pushed me back on an ottoman and fell on top of me. I tried to push him off. He just laughed. After a few minutes of us struggling against each other, he lifted my skirt and pushed himself into me, without removing my panties. Again, I tried to push him off of me, but my attempts were unfruitful. Literally, minutes later, he was done.

I was in a panic. All I could think about was Linda. I did not know what she would say. When we first went into the house and continued our conversation, she was ringing the doorbell, so she could gain entrance. Her boyfriend had locked the door. After he got off me, he didn't have anything else to say except, "Don't tell Linda." I couldn't think straight. All I wanted to do was get out of there, and I was afraid to face her. When I opened the door, she was gone. So, I went directly home and never uttered a word to anyone. Well, not on that day at least.

The next month, my mother, siblings and I went to Arkansas to visit my aunt, uncle, and cousins, or either they were here in California visiting. The morning after returning home, I began to vomit. The night before when we had left Arkansas, my aunt had cooked a large spaghetti dinner. That morning, spaghetti was all over my bedspread. My mother's first thought was the spaghetti had caused my sickness. I must have continued to be ill throughout the next few days because my mother's concern grew. However, she couldn't figure out what was causing my illness, and I certainly did not know.

Subsequently, a visit was scheduled for a doctor. He requested a urine sample. After running tests, or at least one single test, the doctor delivered the results to my mother, and in turn, they both told me I was pregnant. My mother was in shock and disbelief. She could not believe her daughter, who to her knowledge was a virgin, could be pregnant. I did not expect the results to come back with that information. Pregnancy never crossed my mind, for I had put the incident out of my mind.

After they informed me of the test results, the doctor stated I would have an abortion at my mother's request. I said nothing. He asked me if that's when I wanted it. I simply shrugged. I wasn't quite sure what an abortion consisted of, but I knew it meant I will not be having my baby that I had just found out I was pregnant with.

I know my mother made the decision she believed was best for me. And, I do not fault her for that. At the time of the rape, I was thirteen. By the time I had visited the doctor, approximate a month later, I was fourteen. Unfortunately, I never experienced the life of my child developing within me. The experience was over just as soon as it began. Therefore, I never felt the loss or the pain of not having my unborn child. Later though, on several occasions, I did calculate the age of my child. However, that was pointless. The entire experience was just a stolen moment in time.

During the entire ordeal, my mother questioned me about the father. She wanted to know with whom I had been having sex. I told her it was my friend's boyfriend, and she was quite astonished. I did not tell her he had raped me; I did not want her to know I had gone inside his home. My mother did not permit me going into other people's homes unless she knew them. I was more concerned about dealing with her wrath than understanding that a crime had been committed against me. My lie led her to believe I was the kind of person that would sleep with my best friend's boyfriend. When I realized that is what she thought, I was hurt. But, I felt it was too late to tell her the truth, so I had to deal with her having that thought of me although it was the furthest thing from the truth. I would never willingly sleep with my best friend's man.

Ecclesiastes 1:9 says, *"The thing that hath been, it is that which shall be; and that which is done is that which shall be done: and there is no new thing under the sun."* Therefore, the abuse I experienced, someone had already experienced the same trauma before me, and unfortunately, someone else has already experienced it after me. Let us take a moment to examine some examples from God's Word to demonstrate the validity of Ecclesiastes 1:9 and to show how others dealt with abuse.

Please note- the ages of the victims were not expressly given in scripture, so it cannot be certain if they were what we would consider adolescents or adults.

Let's first examine the rape of Tamar, King David's daughter, which is detailed in II Samuel 13.

> *Now David's son Absalom had a beautiful sister named Tamar. And Amnon, her half brother, fell desperately in love with her.* **2** *Amnon became so obsessed with Tamar that he became ill. She was a virgin, and Amnon thought he could never have her.* **3** *But Amnon had a very crafty friend—his cousin Jonadab. He was the son of David's brother Shimea.* **4** *One day Jonadab said to Amnon, "What's the trouble? Why should the son of a king look so dejected morning after morning?" So Amnon told him, "I*

am in love with Tamar, my brother Absalom's sister." [5] "Well," Jonadab said, "I'll tell you what to do. Go back to bed and pretend you are ill. When your father comes to see you, ask him to let Tamar come and prepare some food for you. Tell him you'll feel better if she prepares it as you watch and feeds you with her own hands." [6] So Amnon lay down and pretended to be sick. And when the king came to see him, Amnon asked him, "Please let my sister Tamar come and cook my favorite dish as I watch. Then I can eat it from her own hands." [7] So David agreed and sent Tamar to Amnon's house to prepare some food for him. [8] When Tamar arrived at Amnon's house, she went to the place where he was lying down so he could watch her mix some dough. Then she baked his favorite dish for him. [9] But when she set the serving tray before him, he refused to eat. "Everyone get out of here," Amnon told his servants. So they all left. [10] Then he said to Tamar, "Now bring the food into my bedroom and feed it to me here." So Tamar took his favorite dish to him. [11] But as she was feeding him, he grabbed her and demanded, "Come to bed with me, my darling sister." [12] "No, my brother!" she cried. "Don't be foolish! Don't do this to me! Such wicked things aren't done in Israel. [13] Where could I go in my shame? And you would be called one of the greatest fools in Israel. Please, just speak to the king about it, and he will let you marry me." [14] But Amnon wouldn't listen to her, and since he was stronger than she was, he raped her. [15] Then suddenly Amnon's love turned to hate, and he hated her even more than he had loved her. "Get out of here!" he snarled at her. [16] "No, no!" Tamar cried. "Sending me away now is worse than what you've already done to me." But Amnon wouldn't listen to her. **17** *He shouted for his servant and demanded, "Throw this woman out, and lock the door behind her!"* **18** *So the servant put her out and locked the door behind her. She was wearing a long, beautiful robe, as was the custom in those days for the king's virgin daughters.* **19** *But now Tamar tore her robe and put ashes on her head. And then, with her face in her hands, she went away crying.* **20** *Her brother Absalom saw her and asked, "Is it true that Amnon has been with you? Well, my sister, keep quiet for now, since he's your brother. Don't you worry about it." So Tamar lived as a desolate woman in her brother Absalom's house.* **21** *When King David heard what had happened, he was very angry.* **22** *And though Absalom never spoke to Amnon about this, he hated Amnon deeply because of what he had done to his sister.* **23** *Two years later, when Absalom's sheep were being sheared at Baal-hazor near Ephraim, Absalom invited all the king's sons to come to a feast.* **24** *He went to the king and said, "My sheep-shearers are now at work. Would the king and his servants please come to celebrate the occasion with me?"* **25** *The king replied, "No, my son. If we all came, we would be too much of a burden on you." Absalom pressed him, but the king would not come, though he gave Absalom his blessing.* **26** *"Well, then," Absalom said, "if you can't come, how about sending my brother Amnon with us?" "Why Amnon?" the king asked.* **27** *But Absalom kept on pressing the king until he finally agreed to let all his sons attend, including Amnon. So Absalom prepared a feast fit for a king.* **28** *Absalom told* *his men, "Wait until Amnon gets drunk; then at my signal, kill him! Don't be afraid. I'm the one who has given the command. Take courage and do it!"* **29** *So at Absalom's signal they murdered Amnon. Then the other sons of the king jumped on their mules and fled.* **30** *As they were on the way back to Jerusalem, this report reached David: "Absalom has killed all the king's sons; not one is left alive!"* **31** *The king got up, tore his robe, and threw himself on the ground. His advisers also tore their clothes in horror and sorrow.* **32** *But just then Jonadab, the son of David's brother Shimea, arrived and said, "No, don't believe that all the king's sons have been killed! It was only Amnon! Absalom has been plotting this ever since Amnon raped his sister Tamar.* **33** *No, my lord the king, your sons aren't all dead! It was only Amnon."* **34** *Meanwhile Absalom escaped. Then the watchman on the Jerusalem wall saw a great crowd coming down the hill on the road from the west. He ran to tell the king, "I see a crowd of people coming from the Horonaim road along the side of the hill."* **35** *"Look!" Jonadab told the king. "There they are now! The king's sons are coming, just as I said."* **36** *They soon arrived, weeping and sobbing, and the king and all his servants wept bitterly with them.* **37** *And David mourned many days for his son Amnon. Absalom fled to his grandfather, Talmai son of Ammihud, the king of Geshur.* **38** *He stayed there in Geshur for three years.* **39** *And King David, now reconciled to Amnon's death, longed to be reunited with his son Absalom.*

Rape is a disgraceful and heartless crime that not only causes physical, emotional, and mental distress to the victim but to also the victim's family. Absalom, Tamar's brother, planned and plotted how he would avenge his sister. He waited two years, and finally, the opportunity presented itself. Although time had passed, Absalom had not forgotten the crime that his brother had committed against their sister. Although he did not shed Amnon's blood with his own hand, he certainly was responsible for giving the command.

I am not condoning the fact that Absalom took matters into his own hands. That is the responsibility of those in authority. In our modern-day society, that responsibility rests in the hands of law enforcement. Therefore, when the crime of rape is committed, one should immediately inform the police and wait for justice to be served.

Next is the account of Dinah's rape, recorded in Genesis 34 (NLT). She was the daughter of the patriarch Jacob and his wife Leah.

> *One day Dinah, the daughter of Jacob and Leah, went to visit some of the young women who lived in the area.* **2** *But when the local prince, Shechem son of Hamor the Hivite, saw Dinah, he seized her and raped her.* **3** *But then he fell in love with her, and he tried to win her affection with tender words.* **4** *He said to his father, Hamor, "Get me this young girl. I want to marry her."* **5** *Soon Jacob heard that Shechem had defiled his daughter, Dinah. But since his sons were out in the fields herding his livestock, he said nothing until they returned.* **6** *Hamor, Shechem's father,*

came to discuss the matter with Jacob. [7] Meanwhile, Jacob's sons had come in from the field as soon as they heard what had happened. They were shocked and furious that their sister had been raped. Shechem had done a disgraceful thing against Jacob's family, something that should never be done. [8] Hamor tried to speak with Jacob and his sons. "My son Shechem is truly in love with your daughter," he said. "Please let him marry her. [9] In fact, let's arrange other marriages, too. You give us your daughters for our sons, and we will give you our daughters for your sons. [10] And you may live among us; the land is open to you! Settle here and trade with us. And feel free to buy property in the area." [11] Then Shechem himself spoke to Dinah's father and brothers. "Please be kind to me, and let me marry her," he begged. "I will give you whatever you ask. [12] No matter what dowry or gift you demand, I will gladly pay it—just give me the girl as my wife." [13] But since Shechem had defiled their sister, Dinah, Jacob's sons responded deceitfully to Shechem and his father, Hamor. [14] They said to them, "We couldn't possibly allow this, because you're not circumcised. It would be a disgrace for our sister to marry a man like you! [15] But here is a solution. If every man among you will be circumcised like we are, [16] then we will give you our daughters, and we'll take your daughters for ourselves. We will live among you and become one people. [17] But if you don't agree to be circumcised, we will take her and be on our way." [18] Hamor and his son Shechem agreed to their proposal. [19] Shechem wasted no time in acting on this request, for he wanted Jacob's daughter desperately.

Shechem was a highly respected member of his family,[20] and he went with his father, Hamor, to present this proposal to the leaders at the town gate. [21] "These men are our friends," they said. "Let's invite them to live here among us and trade freely. Look, the land is large enough to hold them. We can take their daughters as wives and let them marry ours. [22] But they will consider staying here and becoming one people with us only if all of our men are circumcised, just as they are. [23] But if we do this, all their livestock and possessions will eventually be ours. Come, let's agree to their terms and let them settle here among us." [24] So all the men in the town council agreed with Hamor and Shechem, and every male in the town was circumcised. [25] But three days later, when their wounds were still sore, two of Jacob's sons, Simeon and Levi, who were Dinah's full brothers, took their swords and entered the town without opposition. Then they slaughtered every male there, [26] including Hamor and his son Shechem. They killed them with their swords, then took Dinah from Shechem's house and returned to their camp. [27] Meanwhile, the rest of Jacob's sons arrived. Finding the men slaughtered, they plundered the town because their sister had been defiled there. [28] They seized all the flocks and herds and donkeys—everything they could lay their hands on, both inside the town and outside in the fields. [29] They looted all their wealth and plundered their houses. They also took all their little children and wives and led them away as captives. [30] Afterward Jacob said to Simeon and Levi, "You have ruined me! You've made me stink among all the people of this land—among all the Canaanites and Perizzites. We are so few that they will join forces and crush us. I will be ruined, and my entire household will be wiped out!" [31] "But why should we let him treat our sister like a prostitute?" they retorted angrily.

Just as in the previous account of Tamar's rape, in Dinah's case, the lust of the eyes and flesh caused a man to lose his mind and proper judgment. Rather than operating in a respectful manner, he took matters into his own hands. Then, unlike Amnon, he attempted to change his course of action and right his wrong. However, it was too late, and Dinah's brothers were hot on his trail.

Most rape cases involve women. However, boys and men can suffer sexual assault as well. According to RAINN.org, while 1 in 6 women have experienced an attempted or completed sexual assault, the same has occurred with 1 in 33 men. The account of Sodom and Gomorrah discloses a sexual assault attempt against men that was preempted. It is recorded in Genesis 19:1-29.

Genesis 19 (NIV)

The two angels arrived at Sodom in the evening, and Lot was sitting in the gateway of the city. When he saw them, he got up to meet them and bowed down with his face to the ground. [2] "My lords," he said, "please turn aside to your servant's house. You can wash your feet and spend the night and then go on your way early in the morning." "No," they answered, "we will spend the night in the square." [3] But he insisted so strongly that they did go with him and entered his house. He prepared a meal for them, baking bread without yeast, and they ate. 4 Before they had gone to bed, all the men from every part of the city of Sodom—both young and old—surrounded the house. 5 They called to Lot, "Where are the men who came to you tonight? Bring them out to us so that we can have sex with them." 6 Lot went outside to meet them and shut the door behind him 7 and said, "No, my friends. Don't do this wicked thing. 8 Look, I have two daughters who have never slept with a man. Let me bring them out to you, and you can do what you like with them. But don't do anything to these men, for they have come under the protection of my roof." 9 "Get out of our way," they replied. "This fellow came here as a foreigner, and now he wants to play the judge! We'll treat you worse than them." They kept bringing pressure on Lot and moved forward to break down the door. 10 But the men inside reached out and pulled Lot back into the house and shut the door. 11 Then they struck the men who were at the door of the house, young and old, with blindness so that they could not find the door. 12 The two men said to Lot, "Do you have anyone else here—sons-in-law, sons or daughters, or anyone else in the city who belongs to you? Get them out of here, 13 because we are going to destroy this place. The outcry to the Lord against its people is so great that he has sent us to destroy it." 14 So Lot went out and spoke to his sons-in-law, who were pledged to marry his daughters. He said, "Hurry and get out of this place, because the Lord is about to destroy the city!" But his sons-in-law thought he was joking. 15 With the coming of dawn, the angels urged

Lot, saying, "Hurry! Take your wife and your two daughters who are here, or you will be swept away when the city is punished." **16** *When he hesitated, the men grasped his hand and the hands of his wife and of his two daughters and led them safely out of the city, for the Lord was merciful to them.* **17** *As soon as they had brought them out, one of them said, "Flee for your lives! Don't look back, and don't stop anywhere in the plain! Flee to the mountains or you will be swept away!"* **18** *But Lot said to them, "No, my lords, please!* **19** *Your servant has found favor in your eyes, and you have shown great kindness to me in sparing my life. But I can't flee to the mountains; this disaster will overtake me, and I'll die.* **20** *Look, here is a town near enough to run to, and it is small. Let me flee to it—it is very small, isn't it? Then my life will be spared."* **21** *He said to him, "Very well, I will grant this request too; I will not overthrow the town you speak of.* **22** *But flee there quickly, because I cannot do anything until you reach it." (That is why the town was called Zoar.)* **23** *By the time Lot reached Zoar, the sun had risen over the land.* **24** *Then the Lord rained down burning sulfur on Sodom and Gomorrah—from the Lord out of the heavens.* **25** *Thus he overthrew those cities and the entire plain, destroying all those living in the cities—and also the vegetation in the land.* **26** *But Lot's wife looked back, and she became a pillar of salt.* **27** *Early the next morning Abraham got up and returned to the place where he had stood before the Lord.* **28** *He looked down toward Sodom and Gomorrah, toward all the land of the plain, and he saw dense smoke rising from the land, like smoke from a* *furnace.* [29] *So when God destroyed the cities of the plain, he remembered Abraham, and he brought Lot out of the catastrophe that overthrew the cities where Lot had lived.*

When someone is sexually violated, it may be instinct to enact revenge. God has declared, *"Vengeance is mine"* (Deut. 32:35). Just as in the case of Sodom and Gomorrah, God will handle the situation- one way or another.

As previously stated, all incidents of sexual abuse can have devastating and debilitating effects. According to the Washington Coalition of Sexual Assault Programs (WCSAP), the effects fall into two categories: short term and long term. The effects are listed below:

Short Term (Acute) Effects

Immediately following an incident (days to weeks), many survivors report feeling:

- Shame
- Survivors thinking they are bad, wrong, dirty, or permanently flawed.
- Guilt
- Survivors feeling that the abuse was their fault. It is very difficult for survivors to place the blame on the offender. Often the abuser was a person close to them that they want to protect. Or it may be that by placing the blame on the offender they then feel an utter helplessness in the abuse.

- Denial
- Survivors saying, "It wasn't that bad." "It only happened once." "I am fine, I don't need anything."
- Minimizing
- Survivors thinking that their abuse was not as bad as someone else's. Minimizing the assault is a coping strategy. Sexual assault counselors should validate the impact of the abuse and that it is appropriate that the survivor is upset, traumatized, or hurting from it.
- Boundaries
- Survivors can be unfamiliar with boundaries, not knowing when or how to set them or that they have a right to do so. Many survivors need support developing and practicing boundaries.
- Trust
- Sexual assault is a betrayal of trust. Most survivors find it difficult to trust other people as well as themselves and their own perceptions. On the other hand, they may place an inappropriate level of trust in everyone.
- Safety
- Often survivors have an unrealistic sense of safety, assess unsafe situations as safe, and perceive safe situations as dangerous. It is important to check whether a survivor is now in a safe environment by asking specific questions: "Is anyone hurting you or asking you to do things you do not want to do?"
- Isolation
- This is a big issue for adult survivors. Many feel that they do not deserve support, that they are tainted, and

that others will not want to be their friends or lovers. Often, survivors from marginalized communities do not want to expose their experiences for fear of bringing further judgment and attack on their community. Many survivors have been shunned from their families and/or communities.

- Amnesia
- A survivor may not remember what happened. In the long-term, if it happened before the development of language, the survivor may not have a verbal memory.
- Dissociation
- A survivor may have dissociated during the sexual assault incident(s). They may describe "floating up out of their body" or "looking over their own shoulder" during the abuse. Dissociation can happen even when the survivor is not being assaulted/abused; an event or memory can bring up emotions which trigger dissociation.
- Anesthesia
- The body is where the sexual abuse took place and many survivors feel betrayed by their bodies in various ways. They may have tried to numb/dissociate from their bodies in order not to experience the feelings brought on by the abuse.
- Physical
- Survivors may have somatic (body) complaints, eating disturbances, anxiety, difficulty concentrating, and physical symptoms related to areas on their body affected by assault.

- Emotional
- Survivors may be very expressive (anger, sadness), disoriented (disbelief, denial), or controlled (distant, calm).
- Cognitive
- Survivors may be unable to block out thoughts of the assault, or alternately forget entire parts of it. They may constantly think about things they should have done differently; emotion and intellect may be conflicted. Nightmares are common. Survivors may also have thoughts of being in a similar situation and "mastering" the traumatic event.
- Other related issues that may emerge are eating disorders, sexual difficulties, physical changes, substance abuse, self-harm, suicidality, anger, and mood disorders such as depression and post-traumatic stress.

Long Term Effects

- Long term reactions include healthy and unhealthy coping mechanisms, which may be beneficial (social support) or counterproductive (self-harm, substance abuse, eating disorders).
- Immediate reactions may persist and change the survivor's lifestyle. This adjustment stage (months or years) may include:
    - continuing anxiety
    - poor health
    - sense of helplessness

- persistent fear
- depression
- mood swings
- sleep disturbances
- flashbacks
- dissociation
- panic attacks
- phobias
- relationship difficulties
- withdrawal/isolation
- paranoia
- localized pain

- These are normal reactions to a traumatic incident. If we look at these reactions through a "trauma lens" then the reactions make sense but are no longer useful to the healing process.
- Some survivors may be diagnosed by a mental health professional as having Acute Stress Disorder or Post Traumatic Stress Disorder.

The primary effect that manifested in my life was anger. I was enraged that on too many occasions a man had the audacity to violate me. I began to lash out both verbally and physically. Below, I have included excerpts from my book ***Unleashed Anger, Anger Unleashed*** to demonstrate my actions as a result of being bound by uncontrollable anger, as well as expert opinion on anger.

As a victim of sexual abuse, I eventually began to have the feeling of being controlled and manipulated. It is a feeling I despise- even to this day. And, anytime I felt someone was trying to control me or manipulate a situation I was in, I would become angry immediately. I never understand why a simple conversation, or negotiation even, to discuss both parties' desires would not have proven to be a better option. Attempting to usurp another's power was and still is my greatest turn off.

From my perspective, someone's attempt at control or manipulation demonstrated the utmost disrespect towards me, and I was determined that behavior would always be unwell-come and intolerable. Thus, anytime I felt disrespected, controlled, manipulated, and unappreciated, I would lash out- and my temper was deadly.

Read the following accounts of my actions during the following incidents. I was truly out of control. The problem at the time was not so much my behavior but my mindset as my behavior stemmed from my mindset. I did not care that my actions were harmful to others and potentially detrimental to my life. I simply refused to be mistreated any longer, and I wanted the world to know. I wanted my voice to be heard. Unfortunately, I was going about it the wrong way, and I was headed toward a brick wall- complete and total destruction lay ahead in my future if I did not change. However, at the time, that was neither my focus nor concern.

Incident #1 *Deadly Weapon Assault*

One day while at the salon having my hair styled, I looked through the front window and saw a police officer going up and down the street, issuing citations because the street did not allow parking after 3pm. I had completely forgotten and had parked there. It was five after three, and my hair was not yet complete. I immediately went outside to see if there was a citation on my windshield. Thankfully, there was not one there. So, before moving my vehicle, I approached the officer to see if it was okay to move my vehicle to another lot. He told me to move my car or he would issue me a citation. Then, he threatened to have my car towed. The added statement was completely unnecessary in my opinion, and it incited irritation within me.

Nevertheless, I entered my vehicle, so I could commence to moving it to the back parking lot. After all, my objective was to avoid a citation and, of course, towing. As I backed the vehicle from the parking stall, the officer suddenly appeared in front of me, yelling words I could not understand. To make matters worse, he banged his hand on the hood of the vehicle several times. To myself I thought, *He has lost his damn mind.* I had no idea what he was saying, and at that point, I frankly did not care. I proceeded in reverse, so I could get out of the stall and re-park the vehicle. On the way, I hit the officer's leg. As a result, I was charged with assault with a deadly weapon. However, the judge said the officer's ego was probably bruised, and he reduced the charge to dry reckless driving.

In the past and even now, I have difficulty dealing with persons of high authority who use their power to their advantage. From my perspective, the officer had given me permission to move my vehicle. Then, he wanted to assert his authority unnecessarily. I had approached him with respect. and he had responded. His added words irritated me. My mistake was allowing his words to get under my skin and causing me to act. We should not allow another person's words to dictate our actions. In doing so, we give our control over to the person.

Incident #2 *Trouble with the Boss*

During my brief employment as an accounting clerk, on one particular occasion, I requested a morning off to go to a doctor's appointment. The appointment day and time that was offered to me conflicted with my work schedule; however, it was the only one that would be available for a long time to come. And, it was urgent for me to visit my physician. When I requested the morning off, my boss told me I could not be excused from work. I immediately became upset and called the district office to speak with his boss. His boss took the liberty to tell me I could not be denied the right to have needed medical services. After speaking with my boss' boss, I took the liberty of attending my doctor's appointment.

When I returned to work the day after the appointment, I was written up. Again, I called and voiced my opinion to the controller (my boss' boss). As a result of my complaint, a meeting was scheduled. At the meeting, I was surprised to find that they had decided to find some dirt on me. But the only thing that they could find was some days when I came in late. In the meeting, they admitted I had the right to go to the doctor, but they also took that opportunity to inform me that I needed to be on time to work.

I felt they were doing a splendid job of being controlling and misusing their power, like the cop in the first account. They had not bothered to discuss with me incidents of my tardiness until I had ruffled my boss' feathers. So, having read through the lines, I proceeded to tell them I was not wrong about my actions and how I believed they were being controlling and attempting to keep me under their thumb, a place I did not belong. I also added if they had a problem with my conduct, they could fire me as a result. Of course they did not need my permission to fire me, but in the end they did not.

Anyone with a measure of power can attempt to use it to his/her advantage. Therefore, it is wise for all employees to know their rights, while at the same time not supplying the employer any ammunition to use against them at any given time. In my situation, I *was* negligent for not arriving on time the few times I was late. However, it did not give my employer the right to bring it up in the present situation because one did not have anything to do with the other. I was expressly told I could not be prevented from taking off work for medical attention, so the late arrivals were attempted to be used against me. I stood my ground and prevailed- although my tone of voice and disposition were inexcusable. Regardless of whether you are right, you must always present yourself in a respectable manner.

Incident #3 *The Refrigerator Incident*

After believing I had been verbally threatened by someone I was in a relationship with, the person walked away with a "take that" attitude, leaving me to take his words at face value. Acting as though nothing had transpired, the person who issued the threat went on with life as normal. As he was bending over looking in an office-size refrigerator, I marveled at his audacity to speak to me in that manner and act as if he was the king of my universe. Thinking I had to set him straight, I politely walked over and kicked the refrigerator door shut, slamming his head inside. I offered a verbal explanation of my action by declaring that I did not appreciate being threatened and said that if anyone was going to get hurt it would not be me.

In retrospect, I realize I could have caused serious damage to the man's head. However, I did not care at that moment. I was more concerned about his threat. I did not and do not take threats lightly. If a person issues a threat, I take him/her seriously and will respond accordingly. In that situation, I am sure I could have responded a thousand different ways. If I had been in the proper frame of mind and not on guard, my response would have been different.

Incident #4 *Telephone Connection*

As a teenage girl, growing up with three brothers wasn't always the easiest thing to do. As it was one of my brother's favorite pastimes to annoy me by teasing me, he went about his daily activity of working my last nerve. Well, on one particular day, I was not in the mood to be disturbed or bullied for that matter. So, as I was attempting to use the telephone to make a phone call or complete one, he decided to interrupt and torment me. I warned him to stop pestering me. He would not oblige. Irritated with his nuances, I struck him on his head with the phone in order to get him away from me.

Again, my actions could have caused serious damage to my brother, and I would have regretted that for the rest of my life. However, at the time, that was not my train of thought. I wanted him to hear my voice and to do as I said. If I said I did not want to engage with him at the moment, that is what I meant. I did not want him to assert his will over mine. So, I felt as though I needed to let him know I meant business and to take me seriously. Today, I know I could have attempted to convince him with my words or remove myself from the situation. It is not necessary to use violence to solve my dilemma.

Incident #5 *Hand-to-Jaw Connection*

This is the infamous case of guy tries to use girl. Well, at least at the time that was my perception of the situation. An ex-boyfriend and I were having a heated argument. When the debate came to an end, I figured I would have the last word. So, after I finished yelling at him for whatever it was I was mad about, I hit him in his jaw, and without blinking an eye, I walked away.

For some reason, I had no fear when it came to being violent. I actually would dare some people to do something to me after whatever it was I had done. I just wanted a reason to continue my destructive behavior. That mindset is destructive and ludicrous. I would never behave in such a manner today-without just cause, of course. The difference is my temper today is not as it once was and common sense reigns supreme! I would rather live with a purpose than die for something foolish.

Incident #6 *A Tap on the Forehead*

One afternoon, after teaching class, I decided to stop by the nail shop to have my fingernails polished. Something went haywire during the course of the visit. I recall asking the nail technician to change the polish or something along those lines. He said something to the owner, and she came over and told me after that day to never come back. I was appalled at her tone of voice and her hand and arm gestures. I could not believe she would treat a client in such a manner, especially when I was not being rude. I had simply made a request because I did not like the color I had previously chosen.

I rose from my seat, walked directly into her face, and told her I did not need to ever come back there. Then, I lifted my hand, placed my fingers on her forehead, and pushed her head back with the force of my fingertips. Her head snapped back and her eyes widened. Then, she began yelling about calling the police and saying something in her native tongue. I walked out, got into my car, and drove away.

It was that particular incident that showed me I was really out of control. I knew I needed help, and if I did not get it soon, I would be in serious trouble. The other incidents had occurred approximately five years apart, but the refrigerator incident and the nail shop incident occurred within the same timeframe. I was headed on a course of self-destruction, and I desperately needed to alter my course, or I would soon regret it.

After all the accounts of my inexcusable behavior, I learned I am extremely blessed on two counts. First, I am blessed because any one of the above accounts could have landed me in jail, the hospital, or the grave. So, I thank God for His grace and mercy. Secondly, I am blessed because God gave me further grace to come to a time of repentance, forgiveness, and healing.

Not only did I exhibit physical violence from time to time, I would verbally explode as well. However, as time went on, I tried to tame a virtually untamable member of my body: my tongue and curb my temper. After some reflection, I wrote the following poem to exemplify the desire I had to be freed from having good and evil exude from the same orifice.

Anger-Filled Words

No matter how near or far, everyone has a story to tell.
When speaking, the hurts and pains are found to dwell.
Deep inside hearts and minds, disappointments can be found.
Oh those things that easily beset us seem to abound.

On every hand and on every turn,
The words that wait to cross our lips seem to burn.
We try to hold them in, but they come flooding out.
Anytime we give them the opportunity when
we scream and shout.

How is it that the tongue can coat but in the
next moment slice?
How can a sweet and kind person instantly be
colored no-so-nice?
All of these are strongholds and devices of the enemy.
But never fear, the heavenly Father has the perfect remedy.

If we seek Him in all that we do,
And remember the race is not given to the swift,
but to me and you.
Those who demonstrate patience, control, endurance, longsuffering, willingness, love, and temperance.

But how can we gain and retain these personality traits?
Or is leading an anger-filled existence our destined fate?
Having us to believe that is yet another trick of the fallen one.
Instead, we should always continue to look and trust in the
Father, Holy Spirit, and Son.

For the trinity has governance over our lives.
And for Them we should sacrifice.
And strive to be in a better state than we currently may be.
And not until then will we be set free.

We have discovered one way for anger to manifest, and we have surveyed some of the various episodes that can result from anger. Now let's explore what the specialists say about anger and how to control it before it consumes and/or controls us.

> Anger is a completely normal, usually healthy, human emotion. But when it gets out of control and turns destructive, it can lead to problems—problems at work, in your personal relationships, and in the overall quality of your life. And it can make you feel as though you're at the mercy of an unpredictable and powerful emotion (American Psychological Association (APA), 2005, *Controlling Anger - Before It Controls You*, par. 2, www.apa.org/pubinfo/anger.html).

"According to Charles Spielberger, PhD, a psychologist that specializes in anger, Anger is 'an emotional state that varies in intensity from mild irritation to intense fury and rage'" (APA par. 3).

Have you ever experienced being provoked to violence? You are not alone; many people will admit that at one time or another they felt angered or enraged by someone's words or behavior. But, what have you noticed that is different about your response and the response of others? For me, I would say that some of my responses have even been explosive. Why is it that some people just seem to rub us the wrong way? Why is it that a particular person can say or do something that bothers you or gets under your skin, but if someone else said or did the same thing you wouldn't be bothered nearly as much, if at all? Why does is it appear that some people sometimes it purposefully? Why is it that we want to lash out at them for their perceived behavior?

Although all of these questions appear to be important, none of them are as important as the next statement. **What others do or don't do should not have enough power to provoke us to engage in violent behavior.**

> The instinctive, natural way to express anger is to respond aggressively. Anger is a natural, adaptive response to threats; it inspires powerful, often aggressive, feelings and behaviors, which allow us to fight and to defend ourselves when we are attacked. A certain amount of anger, therefore, is necessary to our survival. On the other hand, we can't physically lash out at every person or object that irritates or annoys us; laws, social norms, and common sense place limits on how far our anger can take us. (APA par. 5-6)

But why do we find ourselves sometimes lashing out anyway, in spite of what society says is socially acceptable? "Angry people tend to jump to- and act on- conclusions, and some of those conclusions can be very inaccurate" (APA par. 30).

Alternatives

There are several things that we can do instead of retaliating with verbal or physical abuse that stems from violence. After repeated attacks, our "normal" defense mechanism can become thin and our imagination can become overworked.

> It's natural to get defensive when you're criticized, but don't fight back. Instead, listen to what's underlying the words: the message that the person might feel neglected and

> unloved. It may take a lot of patient questioning on your part, and it may require some breathing space, but don't let your anger—or a partner's—let a discussion spin out of control. Keeping your cool can keep the situation from becoming a disastrous one.
>
> (APA par. 32)

I have had this to work for me. But the key is to use patience constantly and consistently.

The converse of using patience and finding out that someone's motives for saying what he/she is saying is honorable is finding out that he/she has less than positive motives for doing what he/she is doing. What do we do in this instance? The answer is still the same- Vengeance belongs to the Lord. Therefore, we must understand that revenge is never justified. "Revenge is a fighting spirit in action. It is a negative emotion, in that it sends the same hormones coursing through our body as when we feel anger. Revenge is a negative response to anger. It serves no useful purpose. Two wrongs don't make a right" (Kramer, Susan, 1998, *Anger Analyzed from a Spiritual Point of View*).

I know from personal experience that becoming angry and wanting revenge is natural. But once you make it a habit, it is a hard habit to break. And it may not be the case that you do it purposefully, but it becomes second nature. And in the end, the result is always the same- it just isn't worth it. Furthermore, the Bible says, *"Be angry and sin not"* (Eph. 4:26). This verse validates anger as a normal human emotion. However, we must not cross the line into sin by taking matters into our own hands.

Let the following poem minister to your heart. This poem was written to illustrate one of my greatest strengths that the Lord has afforded me, perseverance. By persevering through adversity, despite the mistakes I have made, God has also afforded me an abundance of grace and mercy. Remember, you are strong and when you get weary, read Isaiah 40:31 that says, *"But they that wait upon the Lord shall renew their strength; they shall mount up with wings as eagles; they shall run, and not be weary; and they shall walk, and not faint."*

Perseverance

Why is it that I persevere?
Is it because I know that the end is near?
Is it because I refuse to tremble with fear?
Or, maybe because I ignore the negativity I see and hear?

Do I press toward the mark because I think I know it all?
Or is it a refusal to give up or fall?
Or because I give attention to and heed the high call?
Maybe, it's because I've found I'm strong after all.

Hanging out in Jamaica

A Diamond in the Rough
ACT IV

A Diamond in the Rough
By Paul Heath

Oh, how there are so many like me,
But yet, I am unique
Enslaved in a darkness
Where anxiety engulfs me
Crying these black tears, but I possess an internal brightness.
One to be shared upon release from this captivity.

At times, I feel the pain from the process
of wanting and needing to be free.
The darkness chipped away slowly,
Still there is no sense of relief.
I wait with moments unable to lay hold of patience
And scarred with imperfections
I must be freed from this slavery.

Inclusions formed deep within me
Birthed from this burning desire
And stress from the pressure the process delivers

as a weight so heavy
A consequence for banishing this captivity.

Once freed, will I sit in the seat to be judged
by my imperfections and impurities?
Yes, my blemishes you may see,
and some with profound clarity.

Observe what lays on my surface
This does not tell the full story of my existence,
nor the battles I have endured
to fulfill my life's purpose.

I do not seek sympathy nor approval
But understand this freedom I claim
comes with no fortune or fame
Rather with the wounding of the emotional,
Mental, spiritual and physical.
Still, I embrace it all the same.

You, who sits in the seat of condemnation,
Who may judge me
I seek not your salvation
I implore do not see this as a bluff
For my journey has not ceased
But has lasted long enough
I AM MERELY STILL,
BUT NOT JUST A DIAMOND IN THE ROUGH!

After building a wall of protection around myself due to being misunderstood and rejected by some of my peers, the sexual abuse I suffered only caused the fortress around me to become fortified.

Experiencing sexual abuse caused a great mistrust within me towards men, especially old men, not older men, just old men. My newfound perception was they only wanted one thing and that they would do anything to get what they wanted. That one thing was sex, and if they had to talk sweet, they would. If they had to make empty promises, they would. If they had to pay, they would. All in the interest of getting what they wanted- sex. As a result of my twisted thought process (because it did not apply to every man), I was determined to not be used for or controlled by sex. At the same time, I was determined not to be controlled or dominated by a man- period.

My thinking led me to harbor anger as I mentioned in the previous chapter. The anger was cloaked around me like a shroud. The shroud covered me and distorted my true self. The anger caused me to present myself (on occasion) as a person who did not and would not tolerate abuse of any kind: verbal, financial, sexual, educational, emotional, spiritual, or psychological. My exterior was an impenetrable wall. My tongue was sharp, and I was a force to be reckoned with. Furthermore, I would not allow myself to be vulnerable. To me, vulnerability meant opportunities for me to be misused and abused.

While my exterior was a fortress, my interior was calling for my true self to be loved. Although most people viewed me as lovable and desired to be in my company, if I did not trust them, I did not always give them the love they needed, required, or deserved. In order for the true me to find my way out of my shell, I needed the hand of God to move in my life. I needed Him to chisel away all the debris that clung to me that had hardened, to reveal the love, tenderness, joy, compassion, and understanding that existed within me. At the same time, I needed him to develop within me humility, long suffering, gentleness, and extended wisdom.

From all the debris I had allowed to cling to me, I could be categorized as a diamond in the rough: a diamond whose true qualities were diminished. Let's take a moment to understand how diamonds are formed to appreciate how precious and valuable they are.

First, allow me to dispel a common myth, a misconception about diamonds. Most people have heard and have subsequently come to believe diamonds form from coal under very high pressure and high temperature. That is simply not true. Coal, on one hand, is formed from the remains of early vegetation (Four Mine, Inc). Diamonds, on the other hand, are much older than plants, meaning their formation began before plant life was created. So, if plant remains create coal and diamonds are older than plants, then the remains of plants (coal) could not possibly create diamonds because diamonds exited prior to plants.

So then, how are diamonds created? According to Four Mine, Inc., diamond deposits are formed within the Earth's mantle. The diamonds are brought to the Earth's surface whenever an event occurs, such as a violent volcanic eruption. They are brought to the Earth's surface in large chunks of rocks that contain diamonds, and these are called xenoliths. Before the eruptions, diamonds are created in something called a "diamond stability zone." This zone is found in the upper mantle of the Earth. Diamonds need extremely high temperatures to form, which is why this zone has a temperature of over 1,000 degrees Celsius. It's also extremely high pressure. This natural environment for diamond formation is found around 150 kilometers below the Earth's crust, which is extremely deep.

Notice how the passage states diamonds are forced under extreme pressure and high temperatures. During my life, I was always a high achiever. This is an innate characteristic I embody. According to Dr. Carl Beuke in "How Do High Achievers Really Think?" "High achievers are often marked, unsurprisingly, by a strong desire to accomplish something important and gain gratification from success in demanding tasks. Consequently, they are willing to expend intense effort over long timespans in the pursuit of their goals. Achievement motivated individuals are inclined to believe that continued effort and commitment will overcome initial obstacles or failures. [These beliefs] are empirically associated with high levels of achievement."

Externally though, I had constant pressure applied from my mother. She expected me to continuously excel in all my studies. She would encourage me and push me past any preconceived limits- mine or anyone else's. She also expected me to bring home only A's. Her encouragement and pressing strengthened my resolve and increased my tenacity. She did not offer much on how to deal with my peers' thoughts or teasing. Her focus was always on two things: academia and how I should present myself as a lady.

According to psychologist Madeline Levine, "Decades of studies have found the optimal parent is one who is involved and responsive, who sets high expectations but respects her child's auto only. These parents appear to hit the sweet spot of parental involvement and generally raise children who do better academically, psychologically, and socially. The authoritarian parent actually helps cultivate motivation in their children" ("Raising Successful Children," Aug. 4, 2012). To add to the psychologist's perspective, the Word of God says, *"Train up a child in the way he should go: and when he is old, he will not depart from it"* (Proverbs 22:6).

Due to the internal drive of always desiring to excel, not wanting mediocre or status quo, coupled with the external pressures, which stemmed from my mother's belief in me, I was (from birth) a diamond in the making. I just needed the proper amount of pressure and the correct temperature to assist me in reaching my full potential. Furthermore, the incidents I experienced affected my outcome. Their impact can be viewed three ways.

First is the negative viewpoint. The incidents could be seen to have stifled, debilitated, or prolonged my growth. However, the positive viewpoint is believing the incidents made me stronger, further strengthening my resolve.

Finally, we have the true viewpoint. The incidents caused brokenness, and that which was broken needed restoration. There came a time in my life where I had to face that ugly truth. If I had not, I would not be where I am today. I had to literally move myself out of the way and make room for the Master to come in to heal, deliver, and set free.

So, in speaking of the Master, let's begin our discussion of the deliverance process with the Word of God. Galatians 5:16-24 states, "This *I say then, Walk in the Spirit, and ye shall not fulfil the lust of the flesh. For the flesh lusteth against the Spirit, and the Spirit against the flesh: and these are contrary the one to the other: so that ye cannot do the things that ye would. But if ye be led of the Spirit, ye are not under the law. Now the works of the flesh are manifest, which are* these*; adultery, fornication, uncleanness, lasciviousness, idolatry, witchcraft, hatred, variance, emulations, wrath, strife, seditions, heresies, envyings, murders, drunkenness, revellings, and such like: of the which I tell you before, as I have also told you in time past, that they which do such things shall not inherit the kingdom of God. But the fruit of the Spirit is love, joy, peace, longsuffering, gentleness, goodness, faith, Meekness, temperance: against such there is no law. And they that are Christ's have crucified the flesh with the affections and lusts."*

If a person exhibits any of the works of the flesh (negative behavior patterns) that are listed above, it is a definite sign that healing is needed in order for the individual to be set free from ungodly behaviors/strongholds. Once a person is free from ungodly behaviors/strongholds, in turn, he/she can take on the fruit of the spirit as mentioned above.

Being set free from ungodly behaviors/strongholds is a desire for many, both believers and non-believers alike.

However, it has been said believers cannot be “possessed” by the devil. That statement, to a certain degree, is true. However, to promote clarity and understanding, the statement warrants an explanation. What that declaration means is believers cannot be *fully* controlled by the enemy. Demons cannot "possess" a believer, in the respect of complete and full possession. Possession implies ownership, and believers have already been bought with a price. We belong to the Lord Jesus Christ because He bought us with His shed blood on Calvary’s cross. However, that does not mean that we won’t, because we often do, unknowingly give control of areas of our life to ungodly behaviors/strongholds (unclean spirits) by the choices we make. Therefore, *areas* of our life can be controlled when an unclean spirit/stronghold is present.

According to Dr. Erwin W. Lutzer, author of “Can a Believer Ever be Demon Possessed?”

> Many evangelicals—perhaps most—believe that a Christian cannot be demon possessed for the simple reason that all believers are indwelt with the Holy Spirit, thus the idea that a demon could occupy the same space as the blessed Holy Spirit is unthinkable. However, we might be better served to consider it more carefully.
>
> First, we must consider that the Scriptures never speak of a demon “possessing” anything. While many translations provide such language in numerous texts (e.g. Matthew 8:28), the original text does not convey any idea of possession or ownership. In reference to the human body, demons are squatters and usurpers. Generally speaking, most evangelical demonologists argue that the

best way to convey the intention of the Scriptures is "demonization" or "demonized."

The biblical material mentions one instance where a believer may have been demonized. In Acts 5:1-5, we observe the first corruption of the early church. While others were giving generously, Ananias and Sapphira were giving deceitfully. When Ananias was confronted, Peter states that Satan (an evil spirit) had filled his heart. Theologically speaking, this is no small statement, for the original Greek word "filled" is the same word used to describe the filling of the Holy Spirit (Ephesians 5:18). If we maintain that demonization does not mean ownership, then it is possible that Satan had an internal foothold in Ananias' life.

Paul also candidly warns us "not to give the devil an opportunity." The word translated "opportunity" is a form of the Greek word *topos*, which is found in the origin of our English word "topography." *Topos* indicates the idea of place. Many translations clarify by translating the phrase with the word "foothold" or "place." So what is Paul warning us (believers) about? If we willingly remain in sin, we can grant the devil a place in our life.

Furthermore, Dr. Charles Stanley says, "A Christian cannot be totally possessed by demons. However, invasion into the life of a believer is certainly possible and probably more common than we will ever know. Consequently, believers can take on mannerisms and behaviors that are not Christ-like."

How is this possible you ask? There are several contributing factors. First, we (humans) are comprised of three components: spirit, soul, and body. We are spirits that have a soul and are housed in a body. When we accept Christ as our personal savior, the Holy Spirit dwells within our spirit, not our flesh and not our soul. The body (the flesh) constantly wars against our spirit. Our spirit wants to please God, but our soul (mind and emotions) and flesh want to please themselves (Matthew 26:41). When we opt to gratify the flesh and the soul, strongholds develop.

Second, Satan is the prince and the power of the air (Ephesians 2:2). He was given a measure of power in this earth realm when Adam and Eve willfully sinned in the garden. He knows what our weaknesses are, and he loves to tempt us. Does he, therefore, trap us into doing his evil biddings? Of course not. I Corinthians 10:13 says, *"There hath no temptation taken you but such as is common to man: but God is faithful, who will not suffer you to be tempted above that ye are able; but will with the temptation also make a way to escape, that ye may be able to bear it."* We are not forced by Satan to submit to sinful acts. We *choose* to indulge in the sinful temptations that taunt us. But, every action has a reaction. When we choose to indulge in temptations that are placed before us and are sinful, we open the door for unclean spirits to enter in.

Third, we can open doors to unclean spirits by harboring unforgiveness in our heart (usually due to something that happened earlier in our life, such as abuse in childhood, bruising, and/or rejection), or by being involved with witch-craft, such as horoscopes, astrology, tarot cards, fortune telling, or Ouija boards. To determine whether or not an unclean spirit resides in your temple, continue reading.

The characteristics listed in the two lists on the next several pages merit a closer look when they are *pronounced, persistent or recurrent* over a period of time, or *progressive* - tending to become more, rather than less, extreme. When someone possesses one or more of the behaviors from either list, he/she may be calling out for help, demonstrating signs that deliverance is needed.

1. **Confused or disordered thinking:** loss of touch with reality - delusions (persistence of erroneous convictions in the face of contrary evidence) - hallucinations; disconnected speech.

2. **Obsessions:** absorption with a subject or idea to the exclusion of others - compulsions - uncontrollable urges.

3. **Inability to cope:** with minor problems - with daily routine.

4. **Difficulty in making and/or keeping friends:** poor social skills - isolation, withdrawal from society - loner lifestyle.

5. **A pattern of failure across the board:** at school - at work - in sports - in personal relationships.

6. **Prolonged or severe depression:** suicide threats and/or attempts.

7. **Immaturity:** infantile behavior (such as bed-wetting) - over dependence on the mother (excessive clinging as a child and

continuing dependence in teens and twenties) - failure to keep pace with peer group.

8. **A series of physical ailments,** which do not run a typical course and/or fail to respond to treatment.

9. **Neglect of personal hygiene** (disheveled and unsanitary surroundings) or exaggerated concern for order and for cleanliness.

10. **Difficulty adjusting** to new people and places.

11. **Undue anxiety and worry:** phobias - feelings of being persecuted.

12. **Too much or too little sleep**.

13. **Excessive self-centeredness:** indifference to other people's feelings, doings, ideas - lack of sympathy with another's pain or need.

14. **Substantial rapid weight** - gain or loss.

15. **Muted, flat emotions** (absence of angry / delighted / sorrowing reactions to stimuli) or inappropriate emotions (sharp, inexplicable mood swings - silliness at serious moments, unpredictable tears).

16. **Negative self-image and outlook:** inferiority complex - feelings of worthlessness.

17. **Frequent random changes of plans:** inability to stick with a job, a school program, a living arrangement - failure to keep appointments, abide by decisions.

18. **Extreme aggressiveness** (combativeness, hostility, violence, rage) or exaggerated docility (lack of normal competitiveness and self-assertion - refusal to confront, avoidance of argument).

19. **Risk-taking**: taking unsafe risks.

20. **Lack of zest and enthusiasm:** listlessness, sadness, mood habitually down - limited or missing sense of humor.

In addition to the characteristics listed on the previous page, below is a list of ungodly behaviors/strongholds believers can possess. Read the list carefully to see if any resonate with you.

Spirit of anger (bouts of rage) (Eph. 4:26)
Spirit of infirmity or weakness (Luke 13:11)
Spirit of antichrist (I John 4:3)
Spirit of fear (II Tim. 1:7)
Deaf spirit (Mark 9:25)
Perverse spirit (Isa. 19:14)
Dumb spirit (Mark 9:25)
Sorrowful spirit (I Sam. 1:15)
Blind spirit (Matt. 9:27)
Spirit of slumber (Rom. 11:8)
Foul spirit (Mark 9:25; Rev. 18:2)
Spirit of whoredoms (Hos. 5:4)
Unclean spirit (Matt. 14:43; Mark 1:23, 26; 3:30; 5:2,8, 7:25)
Destroying spirit (Deut. 13:15)
Evil spirit (Judges 9:23; I Sam. 16:14-16, 23; 18:10; 19:9)

Spirit of divination (Acts 16:16)
Another spirit (II Cor. 11:4)
Spirit of bondage (Rom. 8:15)
Hasty of spirit (Prov. 14:29)
Spirit of error (I John 4:6)
Haughty spirit (Prov. 16:18)
Spirit of false doctrines (Ex. 23:1; Matt. 16:12)
Perverse spirit (Isa. 19:14)
Spirit of jealousy (Num. 5:14)
Seducing spirits (I Tim. 4:1)
Sad spirit (I Kings 21:5)
Jealous spirit (Num. 5:14, 30)
Wounded spirit (Prov. 18:14)
Lying spirit (I Kings 22:22-23; II Ch. 18:21-22)
Proud in spirit (Ecc. 7:8)
Spirit of burning (Isa. 4:4)
Familiar spirit (Lev. 20:27; I Sam. 28:7-8; I Ch. 10:13; II Ch. 33:6)
Spirit of Egypt (Isa. 19:3)
Spirit of heaviness (Isa. 61:3)
Spirit of unclean devil (Luke 4:33)
Spirit of the world (I Cor. 2:12)

Timeframe for Deliverance

For some, deliverance can happen instantly, while for most others, it is a process. The process can take months, or it can take years. The difference in timeframe is most likely predicated upon one's mindset and/or how long the ungodly behaviors/strongholds have afflicted him/her. If a person does not see a need to be free from the ungodly spirit or does not recognize its existence, he/she will remain bound for a longer period of time than one who desires the ungodly behaviors/ strongholds to be expurgated. If the spirits have occupied the person's temple for a while, it will be harder to eradicate them or the residual effects because the person has grown accustomed to operating in a certain manner and may be fearful of change or believe he/she is the way he/she is because that is how God made him/her. This is a lie from the enemy designed to keep one bound. In order to live a fulfilled life, our temple must be free from all ungodly behaviors/ strongholds.

To better understand how to begin the process of deliverance, read the two scriptures below:

Matthew 12:43-45 says, *"When an impure spirit comes out of a person, it goes through arid places seeking rest and does not find it. Then it says, 'I will return to the house I left.' When it arrives, it finds the house unoccupied, swept clean and put in order. Then it goes and takes with it seven other spirits more wicked than itself, and they go in and live there. And the final condition of that person is worse than the first. That is how it will be with this wicked generation"* (NIV).

Luke 11:25-26 says, *"When it arrives, it finds the house swept clean and put in order. Then it goes and takes seven other spirits more wicked than itself, and they go in and live there. And the final condition of that person is worse than the first"* (NIV).

Both sets of scripture provide a hint of the first step in being free, but they focus more on the details of the danger the solitary act of expurgating an ungodly spirit from an individual can bring about. As you ponder that statement, I am sure it sounds quite contradictory to all you may have heard about expurgating evil spirits from someone. I am keenly aware of this seeming contradiction. Allow me to explain.

Careful examination of these two sets of verses demonstrate the need for an <u>additional step</u> that must be performed *after* one is delivered from an ungodly spirit/ stronghold.

Once a person realizes he/she demonstrates a behavior that is contrary to God's spirit, he/she must take the necessary steps to be delivered from it. Before deliverance begins, the person may find it necessary to fast and pray, as Jesus instructed the disciples who complained of not being able to deliver a boy from an evil spirit that possessed him. Read the account below from Mark 9:14-29.

> *When they came to the other disciples, they saw a large crowd around them and the teachers of the law arguing with them. As soon as all the people saw Jesus, they were overwhelmed with wonder and ran to greet him. 'What are you arguing with them about?' he asked. A man in the crowd answered, 'Teacher, I brought you my son, who is possessed by a spirit that has robbed him of speech. Whenever it seizes him, it throws him to the ground. He foams at the mouth, gnashes his teeth and becomes rigid. I asked your disciples to drive out the spirit, but they could not.' 'You unbelieving generation,' Jesus replied, 'how long shall I stay with you? How long shall I put up with you? Bring the boy to me.' So they brought him. When the spirit saw Jesus, it immediately threw the boy into a*

> *convulsion. He fell to the ground and rolled around, foaming at the mouth. Jesus asked the boy's father, 'How long has he been like this?' 'From childhood,' he answered. 'It has often thrown him into fire or water to kill him. But if you can do anything, take pity on us and help us.' '"If you can"?' said Jesus. 'Everything is possible for one who believes.' Immediately the boy's father exclaimed, 'I do believe; help me overcome my unbelief!' When Jesus saw that a crowd was running to the scene, he rebuked the impure spirit. 'You deaf and mute spirit,' he said, 'I command you, come out of him and never enter him again.' The spirit shrieked, convulsed him violently and came out. The boy looked so much like a corpse that many said, 'He's dead.' But Jesus took him by the hand and lifted him to his feet, and he stood up. After Jesus had gone indoors, his disciples asked him privately, 'Why couldn't we drive it out?' He replied, 'This kind can come out only by prayer'* (NIV).

Fasting and praying assists in developing one's faith and strengthening the power God has given us. The stronger our faith, the greater our ability will be to exercise that which God has empowered us to do. Notice from the verses above, all Jesus had to do was speak to the demon and the demon fled from the boy's temple. Jesus knew the power He had, and He exercised it. This same power was given unto the disciples, but they failed in being successful in expurgating the demon. Jesus' response to their failed attempt was, "*You unbelieving generation. How long shall I stay with you? How long shall I put up with you?"* He was disappointed that the disciples had not yet begun to catch on to what they were able to do with the proper amount of faith.

If you have failed in anything, ask yourself where your faith level is. Do you have no faith, little faith, some faith, or great faith? In Matthew 17:10, Jesus declares, *"Because you have so little faith. Truly I tell you, if you have faith as small as a mustard seed, you can say to this mountain, 'Move from here to there,' and it will move. Nothing will be impossible for you."* Your level of faith determines the outcome of that which you are involved. If you believe you will be successful, more than likely you will be. You may not have the level of success you desire after the first attempt, but if you keep at it, you will eventually succeed. However, if you believe you will fail, more than likely you will. This is called the self-fulfilling prophecy, which was heavily discussed by Robert K. Merton (1948) and has been used by educational psychologists from that time forward.

The Bible, however, had already given us insight into this principle. Proverbs 23:7a states, *"For as he thinketh in his heart, so is he."* Whatever is going on in our minds will manifest in our lives. So, how do we change our mindset so we obtain positive outcomes? We increase our faith level. How is that done? The answer is provided in Romans 10:17: *"So then faith cometh by hearing, and hearing by the word of God."* We are empowered by increasing our exposure to the *spoken* Word and to the Word in general.

In reading the Word, we are exposed to and enlightened by Luke 10:19, which says, *"Behold, I give unto you power to tread on serpents and scorpions, and over all the power of the enemy: and nothing shall by any means hurt you."* When we know who we are in Christ, then we can begin to use the power we have to walk in freedom from ungodly spirits/ strongholds.

Now, let us examine the process of deliverance. There are six basic steps to your deliverance. Take one step at a time, spending as much time as necessary in each one.

1. *Know what is rightfully yours*

If you don't believe what is rightfully yours, it is going to be hard to state your claim. Some of the things you need to be clear about are 1. knowing your sins are forgiven (although Satan will always try to bring up your past failures), 2. knowing you are a child of God and are a co-heir with the Lord Jesus Christ (Romans 8:17), and 3. knowing you have authority over the demons (Luke 10:19).

-You need to understand who you are in Christ.

This sounds simple, and is often overlooked, but is VITAL to your deliverance. If you don't really believe you are who you are, then you won't have the faith to stand on who you are and claim what is rightfully yours. Think about this- if a child has parents who are able to provide his every financial need and desire but he fails to take advantage of their wealth by making his request known, he will not enjoy the benefits. Likewise, if you don't really know you're a child of the King, you won't feel like a prince or princess, neither will you act like a prince or princess. So, how are you supposed to defeat the enemy when you don't think like a child of God should think? If you struggle with your identity, you need to tear down one or more strongholds. Begin by reading the following verses. II Corinthians 5:17 says, *"Therefore if anyone is in Christ, he is a new creature; the old things passed away; behold, new things have come."* And, I Peter 2:9 says, *"But ye are a chosen generation, a royal priesthood, an holy nation, a peculiar people; that ye should shew forth the praises of him who hath called you out of darkness into his marvellous light."* And, Romans 8:17 says, *"And if children, then heirs; heirs of God, and joint-heirs with Christ; if so be that we suffer with him, that we may be also glorified together."* Now that you have read God's position on your relationship/kinship with Him, you should be clear about your identity.

-You need to know your sins are forgiven.

If you have guilt hanging over your head, it will greatly hinder your ability to stand up to the enemy with a clear conscience and stand up for what is rightfully yours. Guilt is a door opener and keeper, and the enemy often uses it as a base to launch all sorts of attacks against God's children. You need to understand the nature of God and how freely Jesus wants to forgive you of ALL your sins. Forgiveness, however, is two-fold. First, in order to be forgiven, you must forgive others of their trespasses (Matthew 6:14). The difficulty most people have with forgiveness is placing blame. If they believe someone is at fault, they believe they have every right to be angry, disappointed, hurt, and even upset. I agree. It is their right to experience those emotions when they have been wronged; however, withholding forgiveness is sin.

You are to have a heart of compassion. A compassionate heart is not a heart that is hardened; instead, it is a heart of love. Therefore, you should love others through and past their shortcomings. In doing so, you can offer forgiveness. Afterward when you confess your sins, God is faithful and just to forgive you (I John 1:9), and your prayers will not be hindered.

-You need to have the correct perception of God and your relationship with Him.

If your perception of God is incorrect, you are going to be an easy target for the enemy. If you perceive God as solely a loving god, you will be confused and tormented when things around you don't go as you expect them (the tragedies and natural disasters in the world). On the other hand, if you perceive God to be a judgmental god who only has a wrath, you will walk in fear rather than reverence (honor). God's true identity is two-fold. God can be best characterized as a just god. He is just because He does what is right and what is best in a given situation. When it is time to love, nurture, and encourage, God does that. When it is time to rebuke, chastise, and judge, God does that. God is always fair, for He is no respecter of persons (Acts 10:34; Romans 2:11).

Let's take a quick look at the Israelites. When the time came for their captivity in Egypt to come to an end, God sent His manservant Moses to Pharaoh to demand His people be set free. However, once the Israelites were freed and entered into the wilderness, they murmured, complained, walked in disobedience to God, and committed sinful acts. Because of their abhorrent behaviors, God saw fit for them to wander in the wilderness for forty years until the first generation died off, thereby not being able to enter into the promise land. So, you can see, one god can have both characteristics of being loving and being able to chasten.

Our God is no different from a good parent. A good parent will feed, bathe, and clothe of a child, all while providing shelter. At the same time, the parent will teach the child how to be responsible and self-sufficient, so he/she can function effectively as an adult. But when necessary, the parent will rebuke and chasten the child. This is for the child's betterment. Proverbs 13:24 instructs, *"Those who spare the rod of discipline hate their children. Those who love their children care enough to discipline them"* (NLT).

-You need to know the authority you have been given by God over the enemy.

You, as a believer, have been given authority over all powers of the enemy (Luke 10:19) and have been given the authority to bind and loose in the spiritual realm (Matthew 18:18). You must exercise your authority through the spoken Word in faith. Just as Jesus cast demons out with His Word, you can also cast demons out with your words, which are backed by the authority that Jesus gave us as believers. **Newsflash!!!** You have the authority whether you feel you have it not, as long as you are a believer. It is important to know that your authority is accessed through faith, and, therefore, the more you believe in your authority, the more of it you will be able to exercise. Mark 16:17 tells us, *"And these signs shall follow them that believe; In my name shall they cast out devils; they shall speak with new tongues."*

You must not take a backseat to the enemy who only wants to wreak havoc in your life. You must stand your ground on the solid foundation of God's Word and declare what you want for your life. Romans 4:17b says, *"calleth those things which be not as though they were."* Just because your present situation may not be exactly what you desire it to be does not mean it cannot be. God holds the world in His hands. He is the Almighty Creator, and He is in control.

2. ***Find the open doors and break off any legal grounds***

This step is one of the most important parts of the deliverance process. It is important to find out what opened the door to the enemy, so you can close it and void their legal right to inhabit you. There are a number of ways they can gain access: through sins, ancestral sins (which causes ancestral curses), unforgiving heart (which blocks God's forgiveness toward us), dabbling in the occult, demonic vows, fear, etc. Find the door that was open and close it. Ceasing the activity closes the door. The longer you engage in a sinful activity, the longer you give the demons permission to inhabit your body.

3. ***Identify the areas of bondage in your life***

It is important to know what areas of your life are in bondage, so you will know exactly what you are seeking to be set free from. Make a list of the things you want to be freed from. Then, try to identify the 'open door' that allowed the enemy to move into that area of your life. When did it start? If you had it your entire life and your parents or grandparents struggled with the same or similar problem, then it was likely generational. Often you can locate what opened the door to bondage if you look back around the time in your life when it started.

When I began my deliverance process, I mentally traveled back in time when I believed my personality began to change from my fun-loving, free-spirited girl to a teenager who had built walls around herself and was always on the defense. To ensure I had the timeframe correct, I inquired of my mother when she noticed the change in me. The age we both came up with was eleven years old. Ironically, that was the time I had been molested by my stepfather. The sexual abuse opened the door to the unclean spirit 'anger' and later to the unclean spirit 'murder.' By acknowledging when the change took place, I had a clear understanding of what caused the shift in my life and what needed to be cleared from my temple.

4. Cast the demonic spirits out

After determining which spirit(s)/stronghold(s) are present, take authority over them by issuing a command such as, "In the name of Jesus, I now take authority over every evil spirit present within me, and I command each and every one to submit to the authority invested in me by Jesus Christ!"

If you can address the demons by name (lust, anger, suicide, hate, fear, etc.), you will often find them submitting to your authority easier because it makes it harder on them to write you off as if you weren't talking to them and as though you have no authority. Demons tremble at the name of Jesus. Recall Acts 19:15 when the demon said, *"Jesus I know, and Paul I know; but who are ye?"* If you don't have the authority in your own name, use the name of Jesus!

If somebody yelled, "Hey you!" in a crowd, you probably wouldn't pay any attention to him. But if he yelled out your name, you would be a lot quicker to respond. The same is true with demons. If you address them by name, it is a lot easier to get their attention. Notice how many times Jesus addressed the demons by name, such as deaf and dumb spirits, etc. (Mark 9:25).

Using your authority in Jesus, command the evil spirits (by name if possible) to come out of you in Jesus' name! Don't be alarmed if you find yourself throwing up all of a sudden, coughing uncontrollably, screaming, etc. If you do, that is a good sign. It usually means they are on their way out!

5. Encountering groupings of demons/ spirits

Demonic spirits often work in teams, and if you identify the strongman, it will help you in figuring out their game plan, and give you a better idea of how to go about casting out certain demons first and unraveling their scheme. This is important, because this strongman is usually the big guy whom you are going after. Once you cast him out, the lesser demons usually follow suit much easier. However, sometimes it is better to cast out the lesser demons, and then deal with their leader after they are all gone because he can no longer play games or hide behind them.

As mentioned earlier, I had the unclean spirit of anger and murder. However, those spirits stemmed from the root of bitterness. Also attached to the root of bitterness are hatred, violence, resentment, retaliation, and unforgiveness. Read below for other demon groupings. Note- This list is by no means comprehensive. The list begins on the left side of the page, continues on the right side and onto the next page.

Depression
despair
despondency
discouragement
defeatism
dejection
hopelessness
suicide
death
insomnia
morbidity

Rebellion
self-will
stubbornness
disobedience
anti-submissiveness

Insecurity
inferiority
self-pity
loneliness
shyness
timidity
inadequacy
ineptness

Jealousy
envy
suspicion
distrust
selfishness

Impatience
agitation
frustration
intolerance
resentment
criticism

Sexual Impurity
lust
masturbation
homosexuality

adultery
fornication
incest
rape
exposure
frigidity
harlotry

Gluttony
nervousness
compulsive
eating
resentment

frustration
idleness
self-pity
self-reward

Pride
ego
vanity
self-righteousness
haughtiness
importance
arrogance

6. Check to see if you are free

You should feel a noticeable relief when the ungodly behaviors/strongholds are no longer present. However, they may just be hiding and trying to trick you into calling the deliverance a success, only to rear their heads later. Pray and ask the Holy Spirit to reveal to you if there are any ungodly behaviors/strongholds remaining that need to be eradicated, or whether the deliverance was successful. The long term effect after a deliverance is usually your best indicator, but when there have been symptoms of the demon (such as fear, anger, suicidal urges, etc.), then I would expect those to be gone when the deliverance has been successful.

Don't forget to consider that in many cases, deliverance is a process and may not occur in just one session. If strongholds need to be torn down, it will usually take. When the spirits leave you though, you should feel the difference and be able to freely walk in your newfound freedom.

As a word of caution, it is easier to cast down strongholds than it is to discipline your life. The key to remaining free is to discipline your mind and actions. Jesus modeled a consistent pattern of spiritual discipline during His earthly ministry- and if Jesus, who is God, had to be disciplined, then how much more should we mere mortals do the same?

Here are five components of living a disciplined life.

Discipline 1: Prayer

> *"About eight days after Jesus said this, he took Peter, John and James with him and went up onto a mountain to pray. As he was praying, the appearance of his face changed, and his clothes became bright as a flash of lightning"* (Luke 9:28–29, NIV).

According to Luke 9:29, prayer changes our outlook. It also changes what we look like to others. What an amazing moment in Scripture this passage portrays! As Jesus is praying, He transfigures in front of his disciples. He didn't change clothes or wave a magic wand, but their perception of His appearance changed the moment He prayed. In the same way, when you pray, change is inevitable. The conditions may not change. The circumstances will probably remain the same. But prayer changes how you respond to crisis. It changes how people see you in crisis. Without prayer, nothing transfigures.

Discipline 2: Fasting

Prior to his public ministry, Jesus spent forty days fasting. And of the five disciplines, fasting may be the most challenging of them all. Food is indeed a gift from God. He provided it for our replenishment, but not our diminishment. And whenever food messes up our faith, we have a problem. Whenever the obsession to satisfy our stomachs becomes greater than our need to satisfy our Savior, then God leaves it to us to fast.

Pastor Tony Evans describes fasting as "the deliberate abstinence from some form of physical gratification…to achieve a greater spiritual goal." I love this definition because it clarifies the purpose of the fast: to obtain a spiritual goal. This slight nuance is what distinguishes the discipline of fasting from mere abstinence. There are a number of ways to fast and various types of fasts. For example, it is possible to fast from pleasures, such as social media, the Internet, sex, or any activity that brings gratification and satisfaction. However, I have chosen to focus on fasting from food because it is generally the most common type of fast and the type of fast Jesus practiced.

Discipline 3: Scripture Reading

When we buy electronic gadgets from the store, they often come with a manual that informs us how to get the most out of our purchase. The manual tells us how to use it, how to protect it, and how to care for it. These manuals are written by manufacturers because they are aware of the gadget's original purpose. The Bible works the same way. The Scriptures are like an operation manual for human life, and God's words help us learn from the lives of others on how to live as He, our Creator, intended. Like the gadget manual, the Bible teaches us how to use, protect, and care for our lives. When we don't read it, we are building a life without having read through the manual. We have a great tool but lack the know-how to enjoy its fullest purpose. It's hard to live out what we don't know. So, we turn to Scripture as food for the soul.

Discipline 4: Worship

Worship is a Christian imperative if we are aiming to be like Christ. It's what Christ says the Father is seeking in John 4. When we worship the Lord, we engage Him with intention and reverence. When we worship the Lord, we concentrate our lives on the Supreme Being. In an age ripe with idolatry and a compulsive need to place people on the altar of our hearts, where only Christ belongs, worship must be a daily part of our lives. In prayer, you can be you. In worship, you can forget about you.

When Jesus resists Satan's offer to bow down and worship him, what He shows us is the heart of a true worshipper. Worship is more than affection; it is the acknowledgment of God's invaluable worth and a commitment to express that worth by placing Him above all else. Worship reveals where our allegiances lie.

Discipline 5: Service

Service is another activity not often seen as a spiritual discipline. But if we are to live like Christ, then service cannot be seen as an optional exercise. Service is a regular practice. It is not only something Christians do to give back to society; it is also the heartbeat and pulse of our call to discipleship.

There is no way we can accurately represent Jesus without emulating His commitment to serve others. Our willingness to serve is an indication that we are maturing in spiritual virtues. It's easy to read a book on humility; it is much more difficult to actually live with humility. Service is a tool that God uses to teach us virtues that can't be learned from textbooks but only in the school of experience.
(Crosswalk.com, 2018)

Walking Into My Own-Past Judgment & Criticism

ACT V

"For as he thinketh in his heart, so is he" (Proverbs 23:7a)

The episodes of anger that were detailed in Act III occurred over a twenty-year period, from approximately ages 15 to 35. The episodes occurred very infrequently at first (every few years), but they began to occur more often, about once a year then to a few times a year at the very end of the twenty-year span. The healing and deliverance process that followed took place over a span of nine months (the time it took me to pen ***Unleashed Anger, Anger Unleashed***). However, after my initial hospitalization (the time spent with the Lord as He purged me), I then had to go into the recovery room, which accounted for approximately another year, as God remove additional residue of my past behaviors and mindset. Healing and deliverance is a process in which one must always be acutely aware of the goal in order to stay the course.

In this chapter, I'm going to digress and continue my life story as it played out on the stage of life after high school. Although I was bound by uncontrollable anger, I continued to walk along the path God had pre-destined for me. My anger may have caused some setbacks I am sure, but I pressed forward, on toward the mark. As previously stated, my desire was to teach. As required by the state of California, I needed to attain three things prior to stepping into a classroom: a bachelor's degree, a valid teaching credential, and passage of the California Basic Educational Skills Test (CBEST).

Just prior to my junior year of high school, my mother, three brothers, and I moved from our comfortable abode in the city of Carson, where we had resided for eight years, to the east side of Long Beach. To say I was caught off guard by the change in scenery and neighbors would be a complete and utter *<u>under</u>*statement. I was simply appalled. But, what could I do? Nothing. I was not asked for my opinion, nor was I paying any bills. Therefore, I had no right to insinuate my opinion. So, for the next two years, I bid my time by staying focused on my studies in the midst of running game on the neighborhood boys and men to prevent from being swallowed alive by all the drug dealers who ran the streets of Long Beach or the wannabees. I was encircled by a new element, and I had to learn the game quickly.

I may have been quiet, but for years, I watched and listened to everything that passed by. I had watched many men run game and had overheard conversations, not to mention I grew up with brothers. So, to avoid being caught in the trap as "fresh meat" in a new community, I dated who I wanted to, when I wanted, without allowing anyone to lay claim to me. After all, I was not and would not permit myself to be labeled as anyone's property although several tried. I was a free spirit, and I made my own rules.

From looking at me, I appeared to be naïve. And, of course, in some ways I was. But, I saw how the males treated the females as though they were property. That treatment was something I refused to engage in. My mother had not raised me with such mentality. So, instead of being treated as something to be owned and treated as a slave, I elected to go to the other end of the spectrum. I had rival gang members pitted against each other as the leader of each tried to lay claim to me. As they threatened one another and fought in the streets, I was planning to leave them all high and dry. Unbeknownst to them, unlike the other girls or women they were accustomed to engaging with, I was on my way to college to solidify my future.

I am not saying I was better than the other young ladies. What I am saying is, I was determined to not allow anyone, and I do mean anyone, to become a stumbling block for me. However, I do realize if I had been raised in a different environment with a different mentality than I had been, my future could have easily been the same as those who then surrounded me. And for that not being the case, I praise God and thank Him for always having a hedge of protection around me that prevented the devourer from devouring me. Oh, the praises of the righteous (my mother and grandmother) availeth much. Even when I committed foolish acts, the prayers of the righteous went up on my behalf and kept me from darkening death's door. Oh, the God I serve is so good. I praise Him in all His majesty, for He is the King of kings and the Lord of lords! He is my righteousness. He is my banner! He is my rock of salvation. He is my way maker. He is my peace. He is my all in all. Without Him, I would fail and falter each and every time! All praises are due unto His name.

So, I resided in Long Beach with my family for exactly two years. I was definitely in the lion's den, but I did all I could to prevent from being devoured. And just as God protected Daniel and the three Hebrew boys Shadrach, Meshach, and Abednego, He protected me. I had a hedge of protection around me (Job 1:10). Then, three months after graduating from Phineas Banning High School in Wilmington, California, I packed my bags and moved to San Diego to attend the infamous San Diego State University.

Well, I was in for a rude awakening. I had never been away from home or my mother before – not to live permanently. However, I was ready for the adventure only because I was ready to get out of Long Beach. I had to save myself from corruption although some changes had come about.

In San Diego, my mother and I were able to locate an apartment for rent. Actually, the apartment housed two young ladies who are looking for a roommate. One had just graduated college, and the other had just entered her junior or senior year. I, of course, was an 18-year-old freshman who was moving with only her clothing. Upon finding the apartment, I also had to obtain a job. I was blessed to find a job the same day I found the apartment.

So, there I was with roommates I had just met and a campus job I could work part time between classes. My next hurdle was to figure out how I would get to school with no car. I had to quickly learned the bus routes and schedules. So, I did. Once the semester began, I started classes and my job. Because my mother was then a single parent of two sons (my younger brothers), she was unable to financially support me and my academic endeavors. Thank God for financial aid. Eventually, I found another part-time job – at McDonald's no less – which was along my bus route. I worked there for exactly one week after which I quit. In my mind, they were not paying me enough to adhere to says rigid guidelines or to deal with the rude and obnoxious manager.

A day or so later, I acquired another job at a spa. The spa has several private rooms, and each room held a Jacuzzi. My job was to clean the Jacuzzis in preparation for the next guest(s). I was utterly disgusted by that job. I saw so many used condoms that were left behind floating atop the water or lying on the side of the tubs that I was sickened by the thought of going to work there. The hiring manager did not have the courtesy to mention to me the extracurricular activities that took place in the rooms. It would have been nice to have been forewarned. Needless to say, I didn't work there too long.

Furthermore, my entire stay in San Diego was short-lived. After only a few months in residence, I wanted out of that town. The school was beautiful, and I thoroughly enjoyed my classes and the friends I had made. While I was disciplined in my studies, my friends were not. All they wanted to do was find the nearest party. I understand that is what most young adults do. However, I wasn't so inclined to partake. I declined numerous invitations to go to parties. It was not my idea of a good time to hang out in strange places where danger could find me while I was so far away from home.

Trust me, I had done some reckless things while living in Long Beach and had placed my life in danger on one too many occasions – mostly unknowingly. At that time, I literally believe I was invincible. However, in San Diego, I did not take that risk. I did not date, and I did not go out much. I do recall attending an awesome concert at the sports arena, but that was pretty much the extent of my outings while I lived in San Diego.

After one semester, I decided SDSU (the party school) was not for me. It was too fast-paced, and I felt I was struggling to keep up socially and financially. So, I decided to transfer to Cal State Long Beach to continue my studies.

Upon embarking upon my studies at SDSU, I had visited a counselor to discuss my four-year educational plan. During that visit, I was given a light blue sheet of paper, which outlined the courses I could choose from, as well as the required courses, to complete my bachelor's degree in Liberal Studies (the degree program for educators). After successfully completing my first semester, I crossed out the courses in which I had earned credit toward the 120 units that were required.

When I left San Diego and returned to my mother's home, I was unable to attend CSULB right away because I had missed the transfer deadline. So, in an effort to not fall behind in my studies, I enrolled in Long Beach City College (LBCC) for the spring semester as well as the following summer before transferring to CSULB the next fall.

While taking classes at LBCC, I met my first husband. We dated for two years and then married. Our union lasted eight years total, which included a six-year marriage, from 1990 to 1996. During that time, our two sons were born.

Also, during that time, I graduated from CSULB, earning my bachelor's degree in Liberal Studies. I used the blue sheet I obtained at CSUSD at both LBCC and CSULB to complete my degree. Prior to my last semester, I took the worn sheet to a counselor to ensure I was on track for graduation. She confirmed I was, and when the time came, I walked across the stage, feeling proud of my accomplishment. Graduating from college with my BA would be the first of three college degrees and graduations.

That same year, I began my teaching career after passing the CBEST on my first attempt. I began teaching at the elementary level and did so for a number of years before transitioning to the high school level to teach English. Just prior to making the transition to the high school arena, I decided to continue my education after a hiatus, which had extended for approximately five years.

When I had decided to pursue my bachelor's degree, I had to choose between obtaining a single-subject credential or a multiple-subject credential. After a difficult deliberation between a single subject-credential in mathematics to follow my passion and a multiple-subject credential to teach all subjects to elementary-aged students, I finally settled on the multiple-subject credential. So, when I opted to return to school to obtain a master's degree, I desired to follow my passion for mathematics. However, because my previous choice to obtain the multiple-subject credential, I was not required to take any college-level math courses for my bachelor's degree.

In high school, I had completed all math classes through pre-calculus. Therefore, none were required for my degree. As a result, I had no math courses on my college transcript. To obtain a master's degree in mathematics, I would need a bachelor's degree in mathematics or at least enough lower-level classes to advance to the required courses for the degree. As I had neither, it would take me five years to complete a two-year degree.

Upon learning my fate, I quickly determined I had no desire to spend five years obtaining the degree, so back to the drawing board I went. Upon conversing with a student advisor, it was discovered due to my abundance of English and speech courses I had previously taken at CSU, Long Beach for my bachelor's degree, earning a master's degree in English Composition would be the best course of study for me. So, I took the challenge, and as a divorced mother of two sons of approximately ages four and seven, I went back to school, enrolling at CSU, San Bernardino.

Oblivious to God's plan for my life outside of the educational arena, for years, I told people I was earning a degree in English by default because the path for earning one in mathematics was derailed. It wasn't until after I earned my master's degree in 2000 at age 30 and had published my first book in 2002 that I began to see God's plan unfold.

Prior to going back to school for the master's degree, I had begun teaching at the elementary level. I taught in that arena for five or six years before being approached and offered a full-time position teaching high school English. I accepted the position and taught in the alternative education program, teaching boys who had been expelled from attending traditional schools in the Rialto Unified School District, for two years. It was during that timeframe when I had gone back to school.

Upon completion of my master's degree, I applied to Crafton Hills College for a teaching position. I was hired immediately to teach Introduction to Speech. I was elated. Crafton Hills College was the first institution of higher learning for which I was employed, and I continue to teach there today-eighteen years later. I only taught speech courses for two terms, and then, I was transitioned into teaching English courses, as that is what my master's is in.

While teaching at the college level and continuing to compose and publish books, I finally began to understand God's plan for me. He led me onto the path of obtaining a degree in writing and a career to teach English. After having done so for a number of years, I became quite proficient at teaching the rules for both composing and speaking Standard English. The skills I obtained enable me to edit compositions as well as compose pieces without great effort.

After publishing my second book with a self-publishing company, I established my own publishing company- CLF Publishing, LLC (Cassundra Lynett Flemister Publishing) to publish my own books according to my satisfaction. After I had published my fifth book, I received my first request to publish someone else's book. It was never my intent to become a publisher. After all, I already had a career as a college professor, and I was grading sets and sets of essays all week long during the semesters. However, it is all in God's plan. After the initial client, I began to publish other people's books, but I refrained from taking my company public.

Then in 2012, after keeping CLF Publishing a secret low-key company for ten years, I opened my first office, and my company went public. In the first month, I obtained ten new clients. That may not sound like great growth for a new business, but for a publishing company, it is quite a lot. To date, after being in business for a total of sixteen years, I have published nearly 200 clients' material (books, plays, and short stories).

In the midst of teaching at the collegiate level, writing books, and publishing for myself and others, in 2005, I decided to enroll in college again. That time, I was in pursuit of the highest degree an individual can obtain- the terminal degree- the Ph.D., which is the doctorate of philosophy. My specialization was Education, with an emphasis/focus in Professional Studies.

Obtaining the Ph.D. was a long arduous process. I studied long hours and wrote my dissertation over a two-year period. In the interim, I had to obey the voice of God, who periodically instructed me to pen several books. From time to time, my mother would question me about my progress on the dissertation, especially when I would pause the writing and research to compose yet another book. To answer her query, I would say, "I must be obedient to God." With my response, she understood.

In 2009, my husband and I flew to Minneapolis, Minnesota (the headquarters for Capella University) to attend a two-day graduation ceremony. It was truly one of the most exhilarating times of my life. On the plane ride back home to California, I proudly adorned my tam all the way. And, no one could wipe the smile off my face.

Stepping back three years to 2006, another awesome event took place: I received my minister's license. I was so very honored to be commissioned by God Himself to preach His gospel to a lost and dying world. To date, I have been in ministry for twelve years. I serve as a minister in my local church and in the ministry the Holy Spirit gave to me: International Women's Commission. As an international ministry, the ministry has traveled to various parts of California, Jamaica, Mexico, Alaska, and Canada. In the future, we will continue to travel abroad as the Lord leads.

As my favorite historical figure Dr. Martin Luther King, Jr. said in his infamous "Letter from Birmingham Jail," "Just as the apostle Paul left his village of Tarsus and carried the gospel of Jesus Christ to the far corner of the Greco Roman world, so am I compelled to carry the gospel of freedom beyond my own home town. Like Paul, I must constantly respond to the Macedonian call for aid." Both Dr. King and Apostle Paul traveled as the Lord led them to deliver the messages He embedded in their heart. I too am compelled to allow the Lord to order my steps, so I can minister to those whom He desires.

Now, fast forward to present day. Let's see what has changed and what remains the same.

During the course of my tenure at my present place of worship, I encountered much of the same attitude from some of the parishioners that I received from my classmates long ago. Allow me to set the context. During my nineteen years of worship in this ministry, I have served in several capacities: greeter, Children's Church Coordinator, Sunday school teacher, Pastor's Aide President, Special Events Coordinator, Living Institute Director, Redeemed Women's chaplain and treasurer, ministers' treasurer, minister, and financial controller. Most of the positions have overlapped with me serving on as many as five committees at one time. My pastor called my name so much I was seen as what I will phrase as the "pastor's pet." No one actually said those words to me, but their disposition toward me allowed me to see what was in their hearts and minds.

Let's make something plain. A survey was done and ultimately revealed 15-18% of parishioners are active volunteers within the church where they have placed their membership. I am in that minority. However, the onlookers who despised hearing my name called were in the majority of pew warmers and neglected to understand why our pastor found it necessary to call my name: I use my talents for God's glory and kingdom building. I don't work tireless hours to hear my name called. I work to glorify God and to get needed tasks completed. All the glory goes to God, not to me!

Instead of wasting precious time and turning up their noses at me, it would be more profitable for them to join in and assist with building God's kingdom. If they were to do so, they would have less time to sit in judgment.

Despite the attitude of many of the congregants, unlike when I was nine years old, I did not retreat to my metaphorical corner and carve out a comfort zone. I stand boldly, with the strength and determination that God has given me, and I face opposition as it comes. And, on several occasions, it has met me directly in my face. Oh, yes! The devil is bold as well, and he will send his imps and soldiers to do his bidding. But, I am equipped with power from a greater source. I am equipped by the Almighty God, the creator of all, and I will never ever bow down, for I am a child and servant of the Most High God, and I will do His will with the right spirit.

Amazingly, through all I have encountered and endured, I have developed a heart of compassion. Was my heart always in this condition? No. Just as my emotions and behavioral patterns had to undergo a transformation, the same was true for my heart. As a child, my heart was tender. However, circumstances brought about a great change within me, and it was not for my betterment or anyone else's. Due to that negative shift in my heart, which shifted my outward behaviors, I needed to undergo reconditioning at the hands of the Lord. That process is called healing and deliverance, and only the Lord Jesus, the Christ, could usher me through it.

Having the mind of Christ, I always attempt to respond in a godly manner and see people as God does. Are their words and actions hurtful? Of course, but I attempt to overlook their shortcomings and treat them with kindness. I strive to be a positive example to everyone, and the best way I can do that is by showing them love. I try not to allow a person's attitude to dictate my own. By remaining humble, it is easier to operate in a Christian manner.

Have I always been successful at maintaining a Christ-like demeanor? No. I am human, and I am prone to err. However, I do not allow my humanness to be my downfall. I strive to allow the Spirit of God that resides in me to permeate my entire being. In doing so, the Lord's light can emanate from me, permeating the atmosphere. I strive to be a sweet-smelling savor unto the Lord's nostrils rather than a stench that would cause Him to turn His head.

Through it all, I have matured physically, emotionally, intellectually, and spiritually. My aim is to let my light shine, as I continue to be the salt of the earth!

What Lies Ahead in My Future?

ACT VI

After having taught for twenty-seven years, published for sixteen years, earned three degrees, been in ministry for thirteen years, and authored thirty-seven books and counting, one could say I have lived a full life and accomplished much. I would whole heartedly agree.

By the time I had earned my doctorate degree, I was well satisfied with my life. All the checkmarks were in place- right next to the goals and objectives. But one day that changed when God opened my heart and poured in yet two more mandates. Both are yet unaccomplished and are magnanimous compared to all else I have accomplished. One is currently in the making during the writing of this book. My deadline is the end of this year. The details will be disclosed in due season. On the other hand, the second mandate will be shared in the paragraphs that follow.

During the time I embarked upon the journey of earning a doctorate degree, I was filled with anticipation of the opportunities the elitist degree would bring to me by having it in my possession. I was unsure of how it would change my life or if my life would change at all. I knew I would earn more money teaching because in the educational arena, one earns more money with each degree or course units he/she obtains. Beyond that, I was unaware of any further changes I would possible encounter.

However, during my first year of the doctoral program, the Lord placed an exciting challenge into my spirit: to open my own school. How exciting is that? I was overjoyed with the idea, but I was quite taken aback by the enormity of the challenge. Nevertheless, I agreed to take on the challenge. But, first things first. I had to determine what type of school I would open and whether or not I wanted to create the curriculum.

After a short period of pondering, I decided I wanted to bridge the natural arena with the spiritual arena, so I decided my school will be a private Christian academy, and I will use the Abeka program rather than write my own curriculum for six grade levels. Why re-invent the wheel, right? When my sons were enrolled in a Christian academy, I was well pleased with the curriculum that was in place.

The next step was to find a location. I began searching for a building in the High Desert. I saw a few nice buildings, but they were not school buildings. They were office spaces that I could easily transform into a school. However, one primary component would be lacking: a playground. I am a firm proponent of children participating in physical activities to encourage healthy bodies from the outside, while eating healthy for the inside and studying God's Word along with the basic educational components to stir the spirit and mind. Eventually, my search for a building ended, as I needed to focus on the completion of my degree. So, that is where I placed my focus.

Over time and after I completed my degree, I had placed the idea of opening a school so far in the back of my mind that I literally forgot. Then, one day quite unexpectedly, the idea shot from its hiding place to the front of my mind.

Now that the mandate has resurfaced, I am determined to bring the opening and operation of the academy to fruition. I am listening intently for the Holy Spirit's guidance and direction.

What caused the idea of the school to resurface? In or around 2015, a friend of a friend approached me regarding being a vendor for the County of Los Angeles, mentioning the various types of training that the many departments within the county contracted out for throughout the year. Some of the topics included professional training, such as grammar workshops and business writing. My curiosity was certainly peeked. During the same conversation I had with the friend of a friend, she mentioned the overwhelming amount of money the county possesses to spend on the professional trainings for the employees.

After that conversation, the Holy Spirit brought back to my remembrance the mandate of opening the school. So, I began to pray earnestly for God's hand to move in guiding me to the right contract and granting me favor in attaining one, if that was indeed His method of supplying me with income for the school. However, a couple of years passed by. During that time, I received two calls for one-day workshops. Although I enjoyed the experiences, those workshops would in no way bankroll the opening of a state-of-the-art Christian academy. So, my prayers continued. Then, I was awarded a large contract that extending for a five-month period. I completed that contract and was recently awarded another one. God is on the move.

During my prayer time, I specifically told God, "I am willing to walk in obedience and open a Christian academy to ensure your children have a solid foundation of all the tools, both natural and spiritual, they will need to navigate successfully in the earth realm. But, I am going to need you to supply the finances." So, from that point, I have been patiently waiting for God to order my steps and to show me the path on which to walk, for the Bible tells me in Psalm 119:105, *"Thy word is a lamp unto my feet, and a light unto my path."* I wholeheartedly trust that if God gives me an assignment, He will give me the tools, skills, and finances to complete the task. Additionally, wisdom tells me it will be done in God's time, not mine.

Meanwhile…

I will continue to teach (in various capacities), minister the Gospel of Jesus Christ, compose books, and continue to publish for others as I await the shift.

50

A Word of Wisdom

Life is filled with the unexpected, and it comes in a multitude of forms: joys, trials, tests, accomplishments, triumphs, tribulations, pleasures, disappointments, achievements, and debacles.

During the course of our life, we should always have a plan regarding our present and our future, so we can fulfill our God-given purpose. The Bible instructs us to write the vision and make it plain (Habakkuk 2:2). Even with vision and having a plan in place does not prevent the unexpected from occurring- good or bad. Read the following scenarios for a demonstration of what I mean.

On Wednesday evening, Matilda went to bed with joy in her heart because she had received a long-awaited promotion on her job that day. When she had left work, she couldn't wait to get home to share the information with her family. She had not wanted to call and tell them over the phone. She wanted to see the looks on their faces. Once she told them, they were very proud of her and experienced the same joy and excitement she had when she learned of the promotion.

The next morning, Matilda awakens to the sound of her alarm and commences the same process she executes every Monday through Friday morning. She promptly goes to the bathroom to shower. After showering, she walks to her children's rooms and wakes them for breakfast. Next, she walks to the kitchen and prepares breakfast. While the food is being prepared, her older daughter goes into the bathroom to commence her own morning routine.

Afterward, she walks into her sister's room to wake her sister up because she knows she did not budge when their mother attempted ten minutes before. Lifting her sister from the bed, the oldest daughter walks hand in hand with her to the kitchen to partake of the breakfast she knows is waiting for them on the counter.

Once the girls are in the kitchen and have begun eating, Matilda goes back to her bedroom, where her husband is sleeping soundly, and dresses for work. Meanwhile, the girls finish their breakfast and return to their respective rooms to dress for school. By the time Matilda has dressed and grabbed a quick bite to eat, her youngest daughter is dressed and seated in the living room with comb and brush in hand. In no more than ten minutes, Matilda combs her daughter's hair and re-buttons her blouse, which was one button off and slanted to the right.

As Matilda reaches for the front door knob, she hears her husband's alarm go off, and she knows she is five minutes late. Hurriedly, she urges the girls outside and softly closes the front door behind them. Quickly starting her car while reminding her daughter to buckle up, she waves to her older daughter who is starting her own car, so she can head to the high school campus. Backing out of the driveway one by one, the ladies drive off in opposite directions. Approximately seven minutes later, Matilda is back on the road again after she drops of her daughter at school.

Feeling a sense of relief after getting through the first tedious set of forty-five minutes in her day, Matilda smiles and leans back in her seat. As she waits at a red light, she flips through the songs on her usb drive until she hears something that matches her mood. The light turns green, and Matilda proceeds through the intersection.

Suddenly, everything goes dark!

Matilda feels pain in her head, and when she opens her eyes, bright lights blind her. When she attempts to raise her hand to her head, something restricts her hand. Then, she hears a voice. Someone is telling her where she is, as she is no longer in her car.

In the blink of an eye, Matilda had been involved in a traffic collision. Someone had driven into the intersection, attempting to make it through before opposing traffic moved. Apparently, the calculation was off.

Matilda suffered many scrapes and bruises, a mild concussion, and a broken arm. She was unable to return to work for a week. Her family had to care for her until she could move around as usual. During the time she was away from work, her boss was kind enough to assign her workload to others in the office to keep everything on track.

Was the accident part of Matilda's life plan? Of course not, but it happened. Thankfully, it wasn't any worse than it was. But, do you realize people lose their life everyday due to someone else's neglect? This part of the unexpected that we must deal with as it comes.

James is a middle-age man who is recently divorced and is a father of two teenagers: one girl and one boy. He has worked for a construction company for a little over twenty years and loves what he does for a living. On Tuesday morning, James pulls up to work and gets out of his truck. He sees his coworkers standing around the worksite and walks over to join them. Some of them are holding travel coffee mugs, and others are munching on breakfast sandwiches or donuts. James had a hearty breakfast before leaving home that morning, so his stomach was satisfied for the moment.

A few minutes later, Devon, the manager, arrives- to everyone's surprise. Devon doesn't usually go to the jobsites unless it is the first day or something has changed in the plans. The group of men and two women grow quiet as Devon walks over to them.

After greeting them solemnly, Devon delivers devastating news- after the completion of the office suites they are currently constructing, they all will be out of work because the company they work for is going into bankruptcy. James suddenly feels his breakfast rising up from his stomach and into his throat. Thoughts bombard his brain. He wonders how he will continue to care for his two children, pay alimony to his ex-wife, and provide for himself. Like his coworkers, he is at a loss for words.

The situation James has found himself in is not unlike situations others have experienced. But, when you have put your time in with a company and performed to your optimal level, you do not expect to suddenly go to work and learn you no longer have a source of income. Eventually things will work out, sometimes sooner and sometimes later.

For any unexpected occurrence in life, we must be ready to shift gears and form an alternate, emergency plan (if you will). Unfortunately, life does not always happen the way we desire, so we must be prepared for the unexpected, which of course is easier said than done.

We should stay in a mindset and attitude of prayer. We must be connected with the Father, so we can hear His voice and receive instruction from Him. We must allow Him to order our steps and direct our paths, for He is the only one who sees the big picture. We don't truly know what our future holds, but God says the plan He has for us is good and not evil (Jeremiah 29:11).

If we trust His Word and stand on His promises, we can make it through any trial and any test that comes our way. Some may be devastating and difficult to bear, but with the Lord on our side, we can make it through.

My life has been a bed of roses for fifty years. (This year 2018 is my year of jubilee.) There is a sweet aroma that springs up from the roses, while thorns exist at the same time that may prick me along the way. I had to learn to enjoy the beauty of what God has blessed me with while navigating around the thorns, being careful to not allow them to prick my outer skin or my inner countenance. Obviously, it is all about trial and error. And, as I came into my own, understanding who and what God call me to be, I was/am pleased with the outcome thus far. Do I have battle scars? Yes. Do I sometimes smell like smoke? Yes. Do I praise God through it all? Yes. Do I give Him the glory that is due unto His name? Yes.

God is an awesome god, and I will continue to serve Him all the days of my life. I pray that you will do the same. If you have yet to come to know Him as your own Lord and Savior, read the passage on the next pages.

Until next time, be blessed in all you do, and remember to keep your head uplifted toward the hills, knowing that your help comes from the Lord (Psalm 121:1)!

Gift of Salvation for Non-Believers

"For all have sinned, and come short of the glory of God."
(Romans 3:23)

This section was written especially for non-believers, those who have not accepted the gift of salvation. The gift of salvation saves souls from eternal damnation and is a free gift offered by God himself.

John 3:16-18 says, "*For God so loved the world, that he gave his only begotten Son, that whosoever believeth in him should not perish, but have everlasting life. For God sent not his Son into the world to condemn the world; but that the world through him might be saved. He that believeth on him is not condemned: but he that believeth not is condemned already, because he hath not believed in the name of the only begotten Son of God.*"

This section of scripture tells us God's purpose for giving His son Jesus to the world. The world was in a bad condition. The world was overwrought with sin; the people were living for fleshly desires rather than for God's desires.

As a result of the world's conditions, God decided He would offer the perfect sacrifice that would save the world from being a place where people were lost and had no hope. He decided that His own son could stand in proxy for the sin-filled world, taking all sin upon Himself.

So Jesus came, born of a virgin, to save this dying world. He walked on this earth for 33 ½ years, doing the work of His Heavenly Father. At the appointed time, He died by way of crucifixion upon a cross at Calvary, on Golgatha's hill. He shed his blood and died for you and for me. Because His blood was pure, it paid the penalty for all unrighteousness and gave those who believe in Him direct access to His father's throne.

Scripture tells us in Matthew 27:51 that the veil of the temple was ripped in two from top to bottom, at the moment that Jesus' spirit left His body. As a result of the veil's removal, we are no longer required to have a high priest make intercession for us. We, as the children of the Most High God, are able to approach the throne God for ourselves, and Jesus sits on the right hand of the Father making intercession for us.

But what is even more miraculous than God offering His own son as the perfect sacrifice was the fact that when Jesus was placed in grave clothes and placed in a tomb, He only remained there until the third day. God would not have it that His son would remain in the heart of the earth forever. In order for people to believe in the awesome power of God and His dear son Jesus, a miracle had to be performed. So, on the third day, after Jesus died on the cross, He was resurrected, demonstrating the omnipotence of God. This very act was the act that would cause people to believe in a god that reigns supreme and holds the power of the universe in His very hands, a god that could save them from themselves.

Today, if you are an unbeliever, you can change your destiny. You can change where you will spend your eternity. Our Heavenly Father gives us the freedom of choice about how we want to live our life here on earth and how we want to spend eternity. In Deuteronomy 30:19, God boldly declares, "*I call heaven and earth to record this day against you, that I have set before you life and death, blessing and cursing: therefore choose life, that both thou and thy seed may live.*"

So, dear friend what choice will you make today? Will you spend your eternity with the Creator or will you suffer Hell's eternal flames? Again, the choice is yours. Just as the men aboard the ship who were with Jonah became believers, you too can make a choice to accept the only one and true living God as your god.

If after reading the above passages, you have decided that you want to spend your eternity in Heaven with God, the creator, and His son Jesus, and the Holy Spirit, read through what has affectionately come to be known as the Roman's Road. This is the road to salvation. As you read through the scriptures that comprise the Roman's Road, you will also read the explanation for each scripture so you will have clarity about what you are reading and confessing.

<u>The Roman's Road to Salvation</u>

The road to salvation begins with Romans 3:23 which declares, "*For all have sinned, and come short of the glory of God.*" This scripture explains that everyone has come short of God's glory and needs redemption. Then Romans 6:23a states, "*For the wages of sin is death.*" Here, we learn that the consequence of living a life of sin is death. Everyone will experience physical death as a result of the sin committed in the garden of Eden, but those who commit themselves to a life of sin will suffer eternal damnation in the lake of fire (Rev. 19).

Continue with the rest of verse 6:23 that says, "*but the gift of God is eternal life through Jesus Christ our Lord.*" There is an alternative to suffering eternal damnation. We can accept the gift of salvation by accepting Jesus as our personal lord and savior. Then, Romans 5:8 says, "*But God commendeth his love toward us, in that, while we were yet sinners, Christ died for us*." We are able to receive the gift of salvation because Christ came to earth and shed His blood for us on the cross.

Continue to Romans 10: 9-10 which says, "*That if thou shalt confess with thy mouth the Lord Jesus, and shalt believe in thine heart that God hath raised him from the dead, thou shalt be saved. For with the heart man believeth unto righteousness; and with the mouth confession is made unto salvation*." If we confess with our mouths that Jesus is the son of God, that he came and died for our sins, and that God raised Him from the dead, we will receive salvation.

Finish with Romans 10:13, which states, "*For whosoever shall call upon the name of the Lord shall be saved*." Call upon the name of God by saying these words, "**Lord Jesus, come into my heart and save me Lord. I believe that you are the Son of God who came and died on the cross for my sins. I believe that you rose from the grave. I also believe that you now sit in heaven on the right side of the Father, making intersession for me. I accept you as my Lord and my Savior**."

Now that you have confessed with your mouth that Jesus is the son of God and that He died for our sins and rose from the grave, **YOU ARE NOW SAVED!!!!** You will spend your eternity in heaven.

The next step is very important- you must find a Bible-based church that teaches the word of God and confesses the Lord Jesus Christ to be the son of God. Don't delay. Do this immediately. Do not leave yourself open to the enemy. Get connected with the saints of the Most High God and keep yourself covered with the unspotted blood of the lamb.

Here is my prayer for you.

Father God,

I thank you for the opportunity to minister your word to the unsaved, the unchurched, and the uncommitted. Father God, I pray now for the souls who have just received the gift of salvation. Lord Father, they have opened their hearts to you, and I know that you have received them into your kingdom and written their names in the Book of Life. Father God, I pray that you will touch their lives and show yourself mightily before them. Let their eyes be opened by the scales falling off, allowing them to see clearly.

Father God, I even pray for the backslider, those who have turned away from you after receiving the gift of salvation. You said in your word that you desire that none would perish. So Lord, I send your word to them right now praying that they would confess the iniquity in their heart, repent, and turn from their evil ways, so that they may receive a life of abundance. You said in your word in Matthew Chapter 14, that every knee shall bow before you and every tongue will confess that Jesus is Lord.

Father God, I pray now that we all come under subjection to your word and that we will humbly submit our lives to you. I ask all these things in the name of my Lord and Savior Jesus Christ. Amen, Amen, Amen!!!!

I will continue to pray for your success in your walk with God. Remember, this spiritual walk that you are about to embark on will not be an easy walk, but remember, the race is not given to the swift but to those who endure to the end.

Be blessed with heaven's best. I love you!

OTHER BOOKS BY THE AUTHOR

(All books can be purchased at www.creativemindsbookstore.com)

From Despair, through Determination, to Victory!

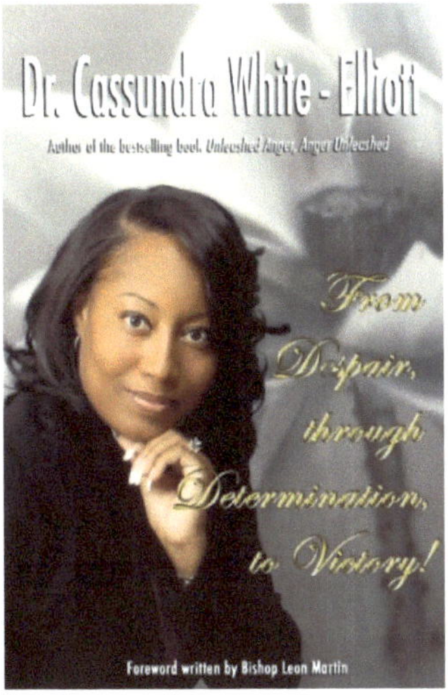

A lot can happen during a span of 40 years. The life of Dr. Cassundra White-Elliott has been anything but uneventful. From a fun-loving childhood sprinkled with incidents of abuse to a tumultuous young adulthood to a stable, secure adult life, she has experienced a full life, with much more to come. Her story is inspiring and motivating.

If anyone lacks hope, reading Dr. White-Elliott's autobiography will propel him/her into an attitude of "Maybe I can." This attitude, if nurtured and developed, will grow into an attitude of "Yes, I can." Throughout her life, Cassundra has always held in her heart the belief that she could achieve anything that she had a made-up mind to embark upon. She was determined to achieve her heart's desires, doing what God has called her to do. She takes no credit for herself. All the glory goes to God, for He is her driving force. In Him, she lives, moves, and has her being.

Through the Storm

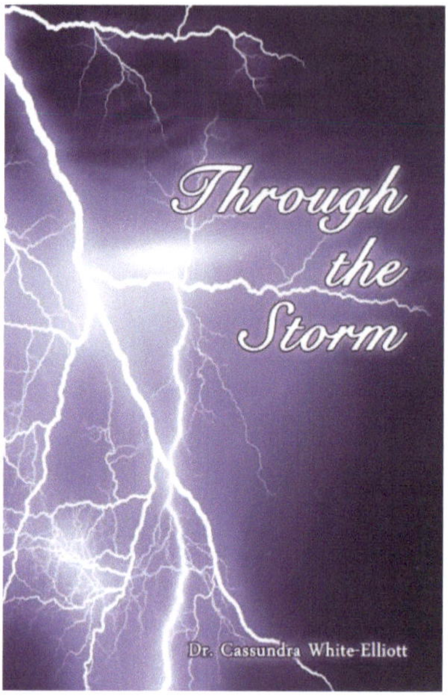

Through the Storm was duly inspired by the avaricious cloud of depression that decided to hover overhead of my daily existence in the latter part of 2007. Although I found it extremely difficult, I was once again compelled to not be defeated by just another snare that the enemy, the trickster, set for me. Once again, or more appropriately I should say *continuously*, he has exerted pernicious efforts to snatch the very life out of me by causing me to wallow in despair and to believe that I had been overcome by failure when in actuality and all reality, I was just experiencing a temporary setback. During those cloudy days, I had to remind myself daily that even though I was a target of the enemy, I am and will always be a child of the Most High god, Jehovah, who is my rock, my stability.

Unleashed Anger, Anger Unleashed

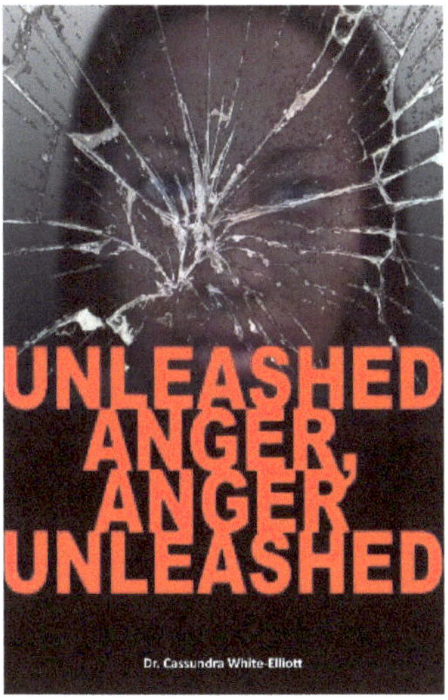

Introduction

What Is This Book All About?

As I prepared to embark upon the adventure of writing this book, I had to prepare myself to also be transparent. I have found that being transparent is required in order for healing to transpire, healing for all those that peruse the pages of this book and myself. And I may as well tell you that today, at the onset of this project, I have not been totally delivered from my condition of being an anger-filled person. However, I am definitely a work in progress. I have made strides with the assistance of my Lord and Savior, Jesus Christ, who is the head of my life. Without his love, guidance, and teachings, I would not be the woman of God I am today. I shudder to think where I could be instead and will therefore not entertain the thought.

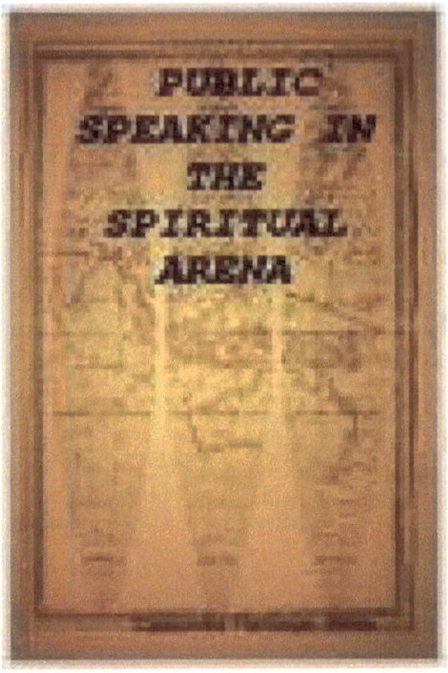

Chapter Two

How Communication Works

Purpose: This chapter will explain the six primary components of communication, identifying their purpose and how they work together.

The Source

In oral communication, the source of information is the speaker. In a church setting, the foundation of the message is God's word, but it is a speaker's interpretation of God's word that is delivered to the audience. As speakers vary, the information may vary but should have a similar essence because the foundational text is the same.

The Message

The message is the collective set of ideas that the speaker (the source) wants to deliver and/or illustrate to the audience. The message can be informative where the speaker informs the audience about a specific set of information. Or, the message may be persuasive in nature if the speaker wants to persuade the audience about conducting themselves in a specific manner, accepting God's commandments, or any number of things.

Where is Your Joppa?

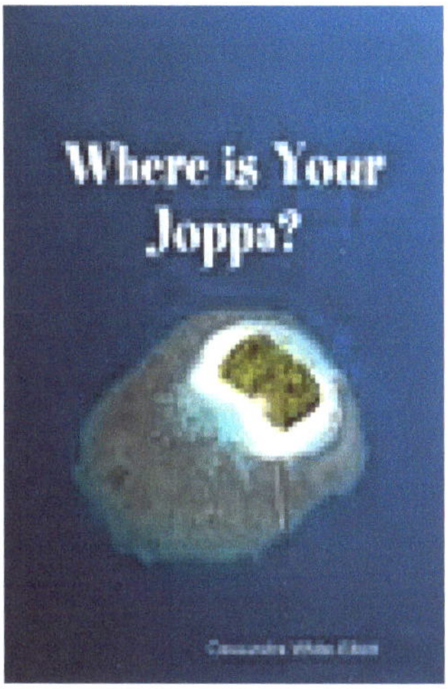

Introduction

Where is Your Joppa? was written for the express purpose of illustrating God's call for obedience in the lives of believers with respect to the individual call that He has on each of our lives. As you read throughout the various chapters, notice that the emphasis is placed on our persistent disobedience in answering God's call in a specific area of our lives. We have become a people who are similar to the Israelites when they found themselves in the middle of the wilderness, following their exodus from Egypt. Before God, they murmured and complained about their current life conditions and failed to be obedient to God's statutes delivered through His servant Moses. Their persistent disobedience caused them to lose the opportunity to see and enter the Promised Land. I ask you, "What has your disobedience cost you?" "Was your disobedience worth what it cost you?" "Do you think about the souls you could have ushered into the kingdom of God?" These are some of the questions that I pray will be answered through your reading of the book.

Mayhem in the Hamptons

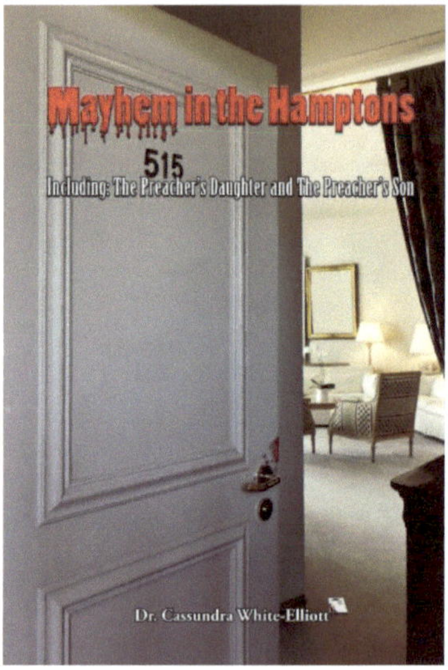

Romero and Yolanda optimistically plan for the day that is going to change their lives from being single persons to a couple who is united in holy matrimony. They, along with their parents, close friends and family, fly over to the infamous Hamptons, where only the rich and famous vacation, to have their dream wedding at the five-star Hampton Suites located on a peninsula in the Hamptons. Little do they know that their perfect day will turn out to be less than perfect when their wedding planner Mariesha Coleman suddenly goes missing!

A time when the newlyweds' lives should be filled with joy and the creation of wonderful memories, they are stricken with grief as they desperately try to find clues to help solve Mariesha's disappearance.

Mayhem in the Hamptons is a tale that shares how the horrors of a woman's past can come back to haunt her in more than one way and the impact it can have on anyone who gets in the way.

Preacher's Daughter

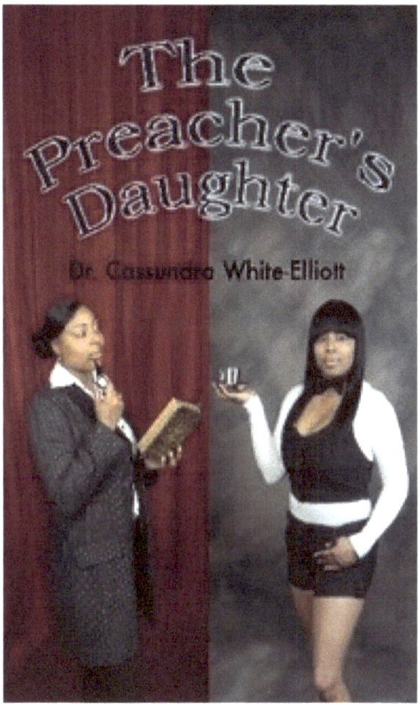

Tinisha, the daughter of a preacher, is a twenty-six year old God-fearing young woman endeavoring to complete law school so that she can make her mark in the courtroom. Working in one of the late-night clubs in Hollywood to earn money to pay her own way through school, Tinisha soon learns that life doesn't always go as planned. Finding her strength in her faith, Tinisha constantly finds herself praying as she watches God move miraculously in her life.

Preacher's Son

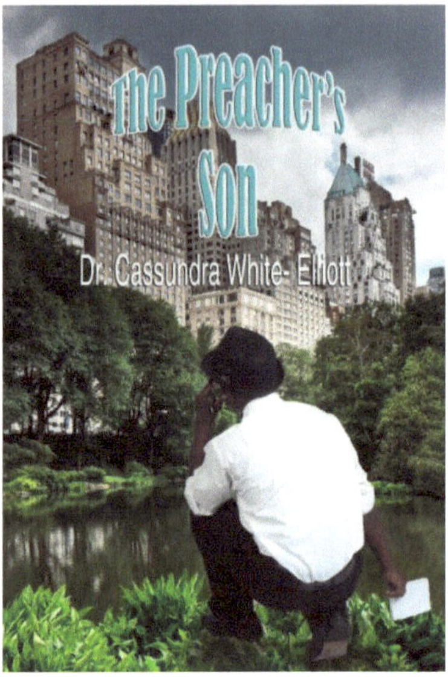

Romero Turner is a private investigator with a promising future. As he continues to build his career, he is excited about the cases he undertakes. However, his father Pastor Theodore Turner has other plans for his son's life. In the midst of trying to save his client's husband from Sylvester Domingo, a ruthless crime lord, Romero must try to salvage his relationship with his father. He must decide if ministry or life as a detective is in his future.

Lord, Teach Me to be a Blessing!

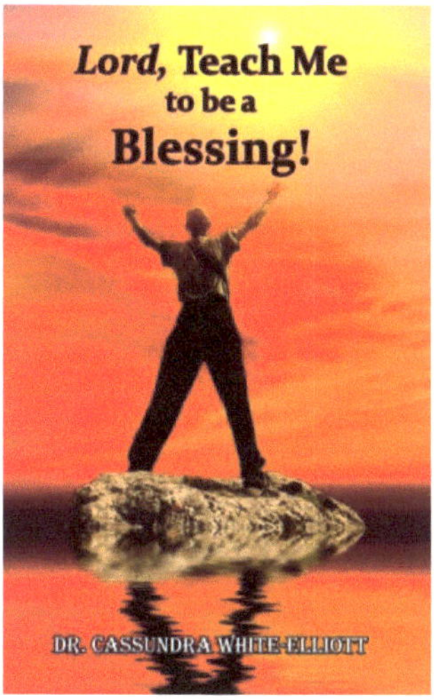

Lord, Teach Me to be a Blessing! will change a person's mentality from being centered around "me, myself, and I" to focusing on "others."

The world system teaches us that it is acceptable to place ourselves above others in an attempt to get ahead and even to survive. Herbert Spencer coined the phrase '*survival of the fittest'* after reading Charles Darwin's theory of evolution. This concept of surpassing and outdoing others is the world's philosophy.

However, the word of God does not subscribe to or promote this self-centered ideology, and therefore, neither should believers. We must hold fast to the truths outlined in Holy Scripture: "*Love thy neighbor as you love thyself*" (James 2:8) and "*It is more blessed to give than to receive*" (Acts 20:35).

While holding God's truths to be self-evident, we must demonstrate them to others, thereby showing them the way of the Lord of how to be a blessing to someone *rather* than looking to receive a blessing. This is the very purpose of this book: to change the mentality of the world from being *self*-centered to *other* centered.

After the Dust Settles

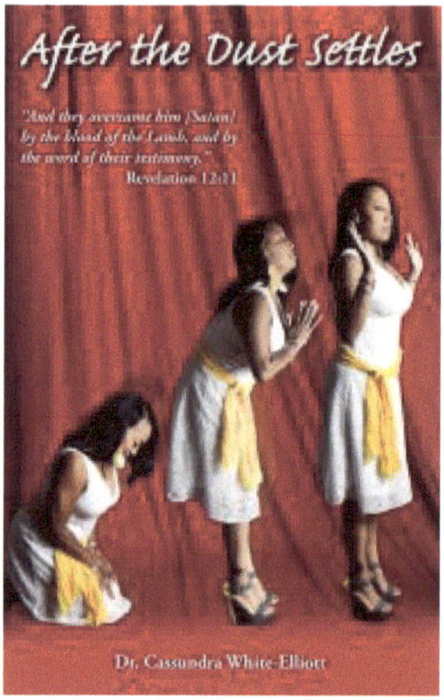

Throughout the journey of life, we all experience ups and downs and joys and pains. Most of us successfully find solutions to the situations/problems we encounter, but we often avoid dealing with the attached emotions. If we continue to ignore the emotions of pain, hurt, disappointment, anger, etc., we set ourselves up for destruction. Our families, our cultures, and our society tell us to be strong, to keep our chin up, and to grin and bear it. However, these methods of avoidance can lead us to strokes due to the undue amount of pressure we place on ourselves and/or mental illness from being unable to cope with the emotional baggage we have accumulated.

In *After the Dust Settles,* Dr. C. White-Elliott shares several situations that we all may encounter at one time or another in our lifetime and how to successfully navigate through them, so we can find ourselves emotionally healthy after the dust has settled and the situation has been rectified.

Begin reading today and experience a better tomorrow!

A Diamond in the Rough

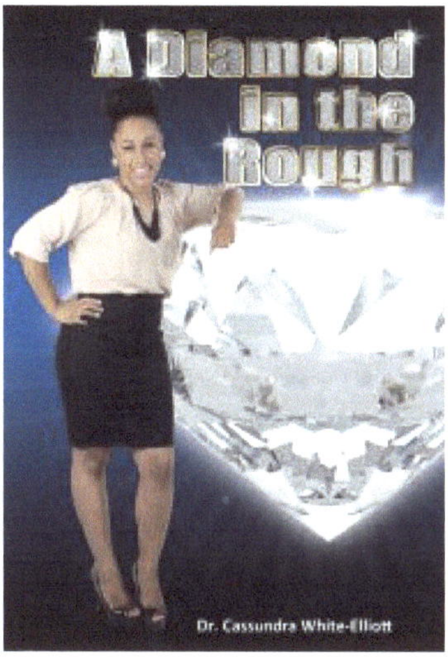

A Diamond in the Rough Architecture Firm was built and is owned and operated by lead architect Kyra Fraser. For the last five years, Kyra has been extremely successful in business, but her love life leaves much to be desired.

Kyra has set high standards for herself and does not wish to take a man in any condition and attempt to make him over. She is looking for someone who is drama free, well educated, very cultured, fun-loving, good looking, self-motivated, and the list goes on.

Will Kyra find the man of her dreams, or will her dream just continue to be a dream?

As you delve into this page-turning novel, Kyra's reality will unfold as you are drawn into her world of design, love and office drama- which includes her best friend's husband who is looking for love in all the wrong places.

365 Days of Encouragement

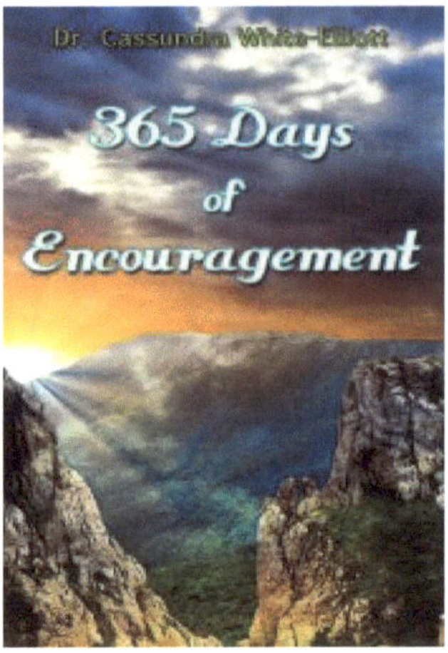

Just as our brain requires oxygen obtained from the air we breathe to sustain our mortal bodies, our spirit requires revitalization and encouragement in order to be strengthened each and every day of our lives. The revitalization and encouragement needed for the spirit of man comes directly from the word of God and assists us in walking according to the way of our heavenly Father. 365 Days of Encouragement provides a scripture a day for each day of the year. Along with the daily scripture is a brief note of commentary also for the benefit of edifying the saints of God.

It is my prayer that the people of God would live a fulfilled life through Christ Jesus. Knowing His word and understanding we can walk in the fulfillment thereof is empowering. We are instructed in II Timothy 2:15, "Study to shew thyself approved unto God, a workman that needeth not to be ashamed, rightly dividing the word of truth" (KJV). Take an opportunity to delve further into the word of God, to know His statutes and to allow your own personal life to be edified, so you can be equipped to bring glory to God and lived a fulfilled life.

A Mother's Heart

A Mother's Heart shares the unconditional love of mothers through a compilation of testimonies. Each testimony serves as a tribute to a special mother. The children of the represented mothers have lovingly written about their childhood, young adult life and/or older adult experiences they shared with their mother. As you read the writers' reflections, you will feel the expressions of love exude from the pages.

The purpose of this book is two-fold. First, it honors those mothers who stood by their children through the trials of life and showered them with unconditional love. Second, the book is a source of encouragement for mothers who may feel inadequate and question whether or not they are actually suited for motherhood. Our advice to mothers is, "Be encouraged; the journey of motherhood may seem daunting at times and you may shed some tears, but your children will never forget the love you have shown them and instilled in them to share with others."

Mothers may not be perfect, but they are definitely unmatched by any other category of person on God's green earth!

Broken Chains

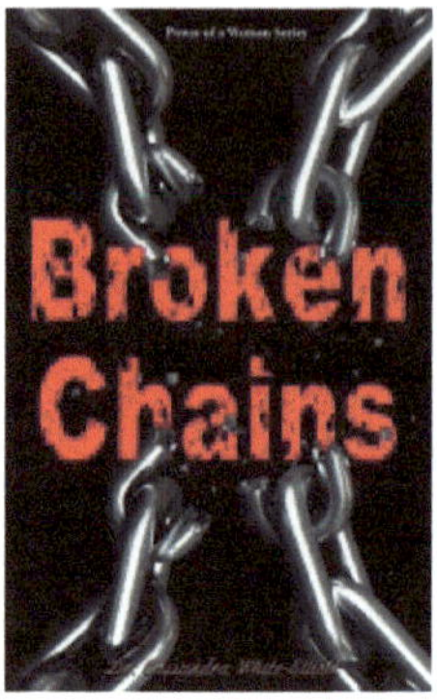

Broken Chains is an in-depth survey of five life-changing tragedies that can and will serve as chains to bind us if we are not watchful and mindful of their potential effects. In our lifetimes, we may all experience death of loved ones, sexual abuse, broken relationships, promiscuity, and sickness and disease. These everyday life occurrences can have detrimental effects on the remaining years of our lives and change our existence, unless we deal with them in a healthy manner.

Broken Chains not only brings to light the detrimental effects of five life-changing tragedies, but it also shares how anyone who experiences them can be healed and delivered from their effects.

If you have experienced death of a loved one, sexual abuse, a broken relationship, the effects of promiscuity, and/or sickness and disease and have not been able to rid yourself of the emotions attached to them or specific resulting behaviors, Broken Chains is for you.

God designed each of us for a purpose, and He has an intended end for us to achieve. In order for us to effectively achieve our God-given purpose, we must be free of chains that bind us. It is not God's desire that we become immobilized by life's events. His desire is for us to be healed, delivered and set free. Be healed today, in the name of the Lord Jesus Christ!

I Have Fallen

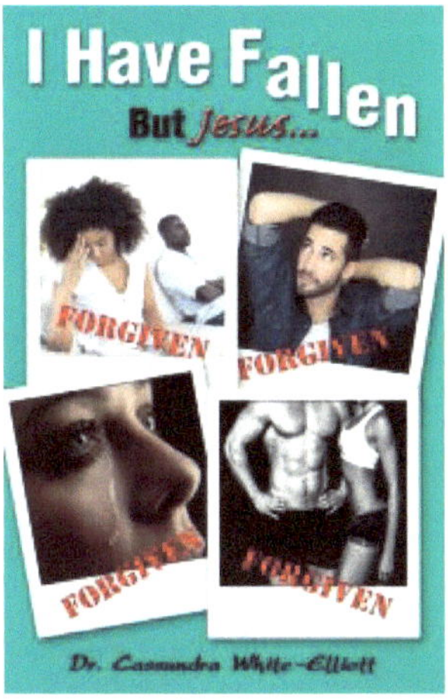

Do you know anyone who has committed his/her life to Christ but has done something unseemly that you would never expect a Christian to do? How did you feel about that person or what the person did? Did you pass judgment? What if that person were you? How would you feel if you made a misstep and no one forgave you and instead began to treat you differently? How do you feel when you are judged for past mistakes or lifestyles that are no longer part of your life?

This book shares four true stories of Christians who have made missteps during their walk with God. The purpose is not to air their dirty laundry, but to demonstrate our humanness and our vulnerability. None of us are exempt from making errors and falling into sin. It can happen to any of us.

The solution for these dilemmas is for the person who fell into sin to make a life-changing move and turn away from the sin, repent and ask God for forgiveness. His arms are waiting!

The next solution is for those who witness the sin or know of it. Pray and be of comfort to the one who has fallen. Lead him/her back to the path of righteousness. Love thy neighbor and treat him/her as you want to be treated!

The Bottom Line

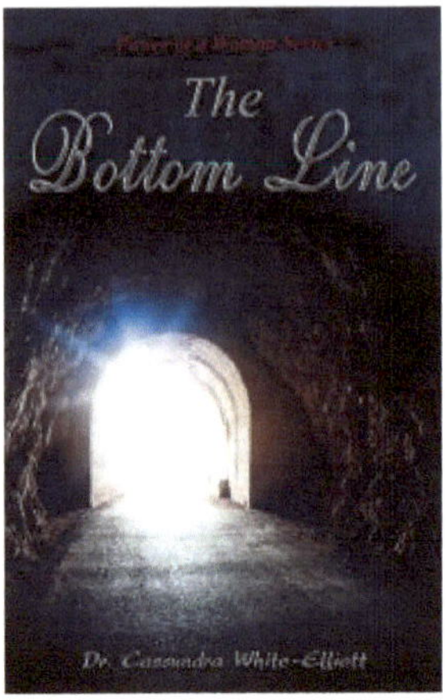

The Bottom Line is a detailed review of the Book of Job. Much can be said about Job's experiences with the loss of his children and wealth and the subsequent return of it all in mass proportions. However, the telling of Job's story in the Holy writ was not intended to focus on the return of his wealth. Instead, the focal point should be on the bottom line of the entire situation.

When you experience trials or tragedies in your life, do you tend to focus on the trial itself, the result, or the bottom line?

"What is the bottom line?" you may ask. The bottom line is the message God is sending regarding the situation.

When Job experienced his tragedies, there was a bottom line. Likewise, when you experience your trials and tragedies, there is a bottom line as well. It is up to you to discover it.

This book will reveal the bottom line in the Book of Job. It is readily apparent, but many often overlook it.

Now, it is up to you to uncover the bottom line of your experiences, for God will not bring a trial to you without a good reason.

Power of a Woman

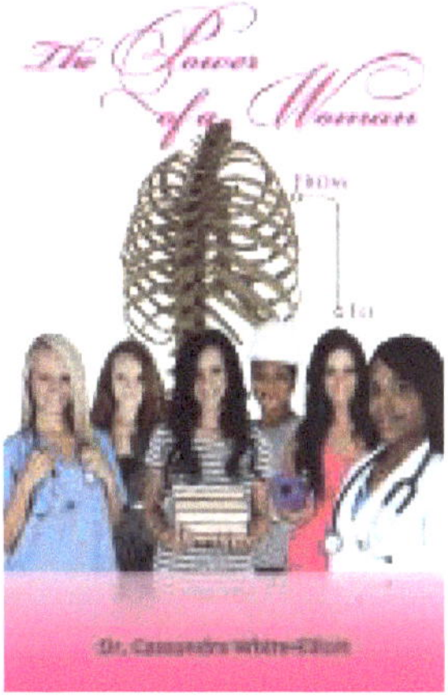

The ongoing conversation about the value of a woman is presented from a different perspective in The Power of a Woman. Dr. Cassundra White-Elliott presents a biblical perspective of women and compares it to the worldview of both yesterday and today. This comparison seeks to illustrate God's intended purpose for His uniquely designed creation: woman. Dr. Elliott shares God's truth about pre-imposed limitations set by man versus the limitations God Himself set for woman in addition to the wealth of liberality He gave her.

Women's creativity and abilities are not meant to be stifled. They are meant to be utilized to bring glory to God, to help sustain and nurture their families, and to move the world forward. Knowing God's truth will show women how to celebrate and appreciate who they are as well as one another!

Women, let's take the blinders off, lift our heads up, and march forward, side by side with men, and bring glory and honor to God! Take your rightful place with a gentle smile and grace and be who God called you to be!

Set Free

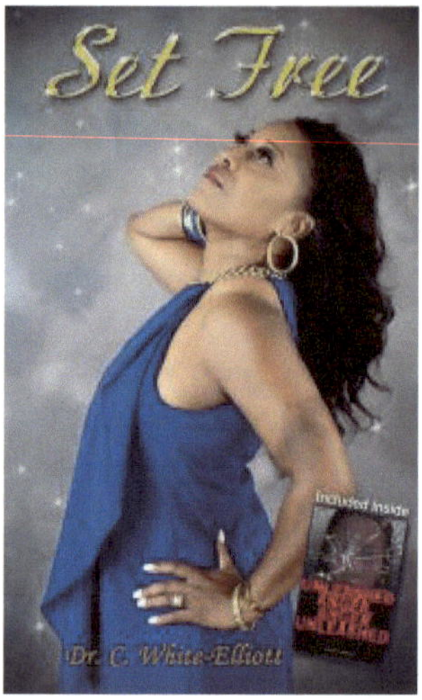

If you possess habits and display characteristics that are unbecoming, debilitating, and hinder the desired progress in your life or that affect your relationships with others, Set Free will provide the steps you need to be healed and delivered, through the Word of God.

Deliverance is available to you! Claim your healing today and walk in victory!

Do You Know God?

Have you or someone you know ever felt alone, confused, or unsure about your walk with God or are you unsure of what being a Christian is all about? *Do You Know God?* is an excellent text for providing answers to many of your questions. This book introduces adolescents and young adults to God in addition to answer many of their questions about being a Christian. This book shares the testimonies of the trials and tribulations that other teens have experienced and how God prevailed in their lives. All the information that is shared on the pages of the book is based upon the Word of God and the scriptures are taken from the King James Version of the Bible. If you are interested in knowing more about God's Word or how to begin your Christian experience, this book is for you.

Daughter,
God Loves You!
"... for her price is far above rubies"
(Proverbs 31:10b)
Dr. Cassundra White-Elliott

Maybe you have heard the proclamation, "The world is going to hell in a hand basket!" Well, I believe I must concur.
However, I do not believe, we- the adult, mature believers- should sit idly by and allow our daughters (and our sons for that matter) to go with it! We must fight for our girls and young women, for they are the mothers of tomorrow, and some may even be young mothers today. Not only will they continue the human race, but also they can have bright futures in their careers and as leaders in our society, as they allow God to direct their paths and order their steps.
Daughter, God Loves You! is a n earnest attempt to address many of the issues that plague our society and turn our daughters' heads away from God.
In this book, we dive head first into topics such as God's love, the importance and impact of education, the effects of social media, overcoming abuse, and the proper perspective of the future.
For the young adult women- Reading this book will empower you to have a bright prosperous future from being enlightened about the dangers that plague our society and how to avoid pitfalls, as you walk along the path God has paved for you.
I invite all of you to take this journey with me to save our daughters and yourselves (young women) from corruption, by being empowered with knowledge.
We must thwart the plan of the enemy. So, LET'S GO!
CLF Publishing, LLC.
www.clfpublishing.org
Dr. C. White-Elliott's books are available at:
www.creativemindsbookstore.com
www.amazon.com
www.barnesandnoble.com
ISBN 978-0-9961971-9-9
90000
9 780996 197199

Web of Lies

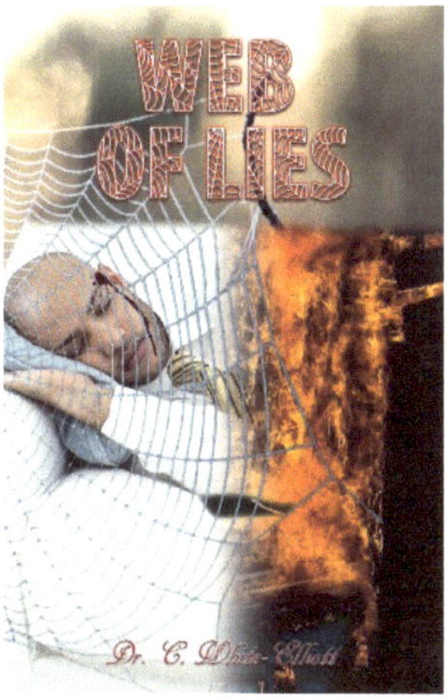

A year ago, Charlito Jimenez was found in his den, lying on the couch, with a fatal gunshot wound in his temple. Everyone in the community still wants to know who is guilty of the unfathomable crime.

Tinisha Salisbury, attorney at law, has taken the case of the accused. Can she prove her client's innocence or will a guilty verdict be rendered?

Halfway through the trial, a badly burned body was found at the scene of a fire.

Is there a string of murders being committed?

Are the murders related?

Web of Lies spins the tales of several characters into one web. Each has a story to tell, and everyone has something to hide. The web of lies, deceit, and revenge take over the lives of these characters to the point where they may not be able to see their way clear.

www.ingramcontent.com/pod-product-compliance
Lightning Source LLC
Chambersburg PA
CBHW040940100426
42812CB00026B/2730/J
9781945102325